LEARNING TO WORK WITH THE TAROT CARDS AND ENERGY AS A LIGHT WORKER

LEARNING TO WORK WITH THE TAROT CARDS AND ENERGY AS A LIGHT WORKER

KERRIE ERWIN

BALBOA.
PRESS

A DIVISION OF HAY HOUSE

Balboa Press books may be ordered through booksellers or by contacting:

Balboa Press
A Division of Hay House
1663 Liberty Drive
Bloomington, IN 47403
www.balboapress.com.au
1-(877) 407-4847

ISBN: 978-1-4525-1074-3 (sc)
ISBN: 978-1-4525-1075-0 (e)

Printed in the United States of America

Balboa Press rev. date: 06/27/2013

Contents

Introduction

Ever since I can remember, I have seen spirit people and had psychic awareness. Sometimes I wonder if I have brought my gifts through from other lifetimes because from the age of eight I was seeing spirit people everywhere and always *knew* when certain events or things were going to happen before anyone else did. At first I thought everyone was like me. But I learnt very quickly that this was not the case and to keep my premonitions and thoughts to myself so as not to be ridiculed or to scare anyone.

I also was drawn to sacred divination, including coffee cup readings, flower readings, crystal ball reading, and the *art* of tarot reading. If practiced regularly, these arts can be developed by everyone to some level. Psychic abilities can be improved, especially if you meditate, because this practice will get you in contact with your higher self (your soul energy) and your loving guides and angels.

I received my first pack of tarot cards when I was only eighteen years old and have never looked back. I was drawn to them from the first time I saw them, and I am convinced I must have used them in a past life. The cards seemed so familiar, as if I half-remembered them. It wasn't long before I could read them for my friends, who to this day are always amused at their accuracy and by the in-depth information I give them. By weaving all the beautiful images and pictures together from your tarot pack, you too will be become a storyteller, not only for yourself, but also for all your friends, family, and clients.

Tarot cards have been with us for centuries. I always have two packs. One is for me alone, and this pack is sacred to me, as only my own vibrations are on the cards. The other pack is one I keep for family, friends, and clients. The cards are not evil, as some people say, because you are only drawing on information from your own divine inner truth and knowing on a soul level. People who have this belief are only coming from fear, which in reality is misinformation.

You do not have to be a gypsy or a magician to read the cards. I personally have always been drawn to use the mythic tarot deck, as I love the design and have had these beautiful cards for years, even though I have had quite a few different decks. I also like the Salvador Dali tarot cards that I bought in New York. Many card readers I know also like to work with the Rider-Waite cards, but it is up to you and whatever feels best and most comfortable.

With my hands-on approach and many years in the industry working as a healer, medium, and clairvoyant, let me introduce you to a wonderful and enlightening journey of self-discovery. Remember that tarot is simply a tool for divination. Like everything else, it can be used for working in the light, analyzing problems, clarifying decisions, and helping you on your life path, giving you more insight about yourself and others. Get to know yourself and others a lot better and allow the cards to take you on a journey of self-discovery.

MEDITATION

Meditation it is an essential tool to help us discover who we are as eternal souls and grow spiritually. It is important for us to see within our hearts and connect with our souls' energy to work with those on the other side in the spirit world. You will always be drawn to people and teachers who will help you learn, but at the end of the day it is your own spiritual guide that will in the long term show you the way to reach higher vibrations. Earth teachers can only show and teach us so much. This process does get easier, and the technique can be mastered. Daily practice and dedication with meditation are needed to encourage communication with our loving guides, angels, and spirit helpers living in the spirit world so that they will help us on our life journeys.

Meditation is not only a wonderful process for self-discovery, but it is also the key to good health and well-being because it brings balance and harmony into our lives. Many successful people in the world meditate and are able to focus clearly and achieve their desired outcomes. By going within and using meditation, we are able to manifest and create our own reality to fulfill our dreams. Just twenty minutes of meditation a day is equivalent to four hours of sleep on the theta level of the brain.

With the energy on the planet now, everything is changing around us as we move into the fifth dimension or what is called the *Age of Aquarius*. This involves a quickening process, so everything appears to be amplified. To support this process, we send love, light, and healing to not only ourselves but everyone we know as well as our planet. When you meditate, call on the light to help lift your light body so it will make easier energetically to go with the new energies coming in on the planet now. Daily meditation helps you to ground yourself to these new energies. It is also a time to take charge and be aware of negative thought forms because they can attract negative people or destructive situations if they are not deleted or dealt with.

When you finish your meditation for the day, it is always a good thing to always close down your energy by imagining your chakras closing down like little lights. It is also a good thing to send healing, forgiveness and gratitude and to all the people in your life, this includes your enemies as this will help you move on. When we are working in groups, we connect with what is called the *over-soul*. This is a collective group in the spirit world that includes all our guides and higher selves joined together as one. When people leave one of my groups, I will always cut them off from this energy so they are no longer connected to the group metaphysically.

Creating a Space for Meditation

For meditation, find a place where you feel safe and secure and where no one can interrupt you. Creating a small space in your home would be ideal. I always make a point to remember to meditate at the same time every day for better results. When you do this, you are also making a date with your own guide and spirit helpers. Once a day would suffice, but twice a day would be even better.

Creating an Altar

On a small table or bench, place fresh flowers, pictures, statues, crystals, rocks, shells, feathers, icons, an incense burner or candles, or whatever takes your fancy. Ask your angels to join you as you create this special and beautiful work of art. Use incense or essential oils for a special aroma to relax when you meditate. Recommended essential oils are Sandalwood, Rose, Geranium and frankincense. Do whatever makes you feel comfortable. Playing harp, flute music or even ringing bells attracts loving angels into your sacred space, but any calming, relaxing music will do.

Creating a Sacred Space in Nature

This is an ideal place to connect to the divine source, whether it is in the bush, at the beach, or in a beautiful garden full of flowers and trees. Here we can get help from the elemental kingdom, which is composed of tiny nature spirits that have been with us since the beginning of time. The undines are beautiful water spirits, graceful little creatures that live around rocky pools and are winged beings called fairies. The tiny air spirits are called sylphs and are full of ideas and inspiration. The salamanders are fire spirits, and lastly we have the earth spirits, which are called gnomes, goblins, elves, and pixies.

If we are unable to utilize our own sacred space, we can simply connect by surrounding ourselves with light and take five or ten minutes to relax, raise our consciousness, and connect with the divine source. A small prayer is a good way to begin. As you begin to meditate on a daily basis, you begin to realize what an important tool meditation really is. Not only will you look and feel a lot better and have more energy, but you will also begin to wonder exactly how you ever coped without it. You will have more clarity and a clearer perception and be able to focus a lot better on all aspects of your life.

Creating a Space in Your Mind

Meditation on a daily basis can be useful in many ways. We can use it for self-healing or sending absent or distant healing to others (first requesting permission in our minds from the person you are sending healing to). If you get a no, don't send it as it is going against universal laws. If you get a positive reply, then go ahead. You can also use meditation to get a stronger connection with your guides, angelic helpers, and loved ones on the other side as you will receive loving messages and guidance.

Regular meditation can also help us manifest our dreams and the things we require in the world as long as what we're asking for does not hurt others. Being successful with this takes practice and dedication. Commit to meditation at the same time every day, and you will over time develop the habit and make it part of your life. Here is a fun script I have written and used over the years.

Manifestation Room

1) Sit in a comfortable position.
2) Take three deep breaths in and out and see yourself letting go of any negativity, cords, darkness, or blockages from your body.
3) Slowly visualize a golden light of love and pure energy radiating around your whole body, making you feel safe, protected, and secure.
4) Visualize roots or plants coming out of the bottom of your feet and slowly travelling down to the earth star and anchoring your energy there.
5) Raising your consciousness and breathing steadily, visualize your energy coming up your body—first as a beautiful red colour, then orange followed by yellow, slowly up to green and then to aqua blue and then to indigo and to purple and then finally up to the golden transpersonal point and feel that all your energy points are aligned. Once you reach the final energy point or chakra (called the transpersonal point), which sits five centimeters above your crown chakra, you can imagine all your chakras are now all in alignment like a beautiful bow which is the colour of a rainbow.
6) Now imagine you have come to a solid white door, which you slowly open. You begin to walk down twelve stairs, counting each one as you descend— one, two, three, four, five, six, seven, eight, nine, ten, eleven, twelve.
7) Reaching the bottom step, you move forward into a long corridor flooded with beautiful golden and purple light until you come to a large cave. This is your manifestation room.

8) As you step into the room, two of your guides welcome you. They are here to work with you and offer you assistance, love, and encouragement. They can be friends, deceased loved ones who have passed over the veil, or guides from this world or other worlds. They can also be from the elemental kingdom or animal kingdom. Now it is time to have some fun and to decorate your manifestation room. Using your imagination, see how creative you really can be.

9) Make your room whatever size you would like so long as it is comfortable and ideal for you. Leave the far wall open for the Christ energy and any healing angels, guides, and nature and animal spirits to be with you as well. For example, perhaps you could colour the walls a soft, calming green, a beautiful pink, or a vibrant blue. Or maybe you will add windows that allow you a view of clear and blue water to add power to your healing, or if you prefer, you could add a beautiful forest of lush vegetation. When you use your incredible imagination, there is absolutely no limit to what you can do. Piece by piece; decorate your room with your own vision of artwork, plants, candles, flowers, and other décor you really love. Don't forget to place an exquisite rug on the floor. The more details and personal touches you give to your room, the more real it will seem to you. Take your time to make it just perfect for you.

10) Near the open wall, create a large screen with neon light all around it. This is your screen of life. Next to it stands a table on which rests a large computer connected to the screen of life. Here you can manifest

your heart's desire by typing in what you want on your computer. Be careful what you ask for. When you are writing what you want, think of an emotional recall of a happy event to make it even more powerful.

11) Sit down and write your script of your heart's desire and what you want to create in your own life. Take your time, and when you have finished, the lights around the screen will be activated and flash brightly as they record and send out to the universe your dreams, making them a reality.

12) After you have finished writing your script, it is time to visit the healing chamber, which is on the right side of your desk. This looks something like a stained glass shower. When you are ready, walk over to the chamber, step in, and simply press the green button on the wall. Now see and feel pure healing and loving energy pouring in and swirling all around you, sinking deep into your skin, healing and soothing you. Now it pours into your mouth, nose, and throat and down into your bloodstream, your lungs, and all the systems of your body, including your skeletal system. Finally this loving and healing force makes its way into your DNA. Feel this pure, white energy penetrate your mind and body, entering deep inside you so you feel the beautiful rays cleansing your body, mind, soul, and spirit. When you have finished your healing shower, press the red button on the wall and take time to enjoy how wonderful you feel.

13) It is nearly time to leave your manifestation room. But before you do, your guides point out to you the time travel machine, which sits on the other side of the room. This machine can only be used by you,

and you can use it to visit anyone anytime or simply travel to where you want to go. It looks like a round silver dome, and you can open it and just sit inside. Once inside you are able to travel anywhere in the world regardless of time and space. Maybe you want to travel to the future or revisit the past or maybe even a past life in the ancient city of Atlantis. Just touch the green button to go. Once you have done this, describe to yourself what it feels like. Notice the sensations, smells, and feels of objects you want to look at. Look at the people. Is there anyone who you know? What are your feelings about this place? Have you had a past life there? Now ask your higher self if you can download whatever you might need from there to help you in this lifetime.

14) You are now ready to come back, and you will remember everything you have seen. Your guides are now by your side, and they escort you back to the door of the manifestation room.

15) You say goodbye as you have completed your work for now. Everything you have done today is for your highest good only.

16) Waving farewell, you slowly begin to walk back up the stairs, counting backwards as you go—twelve, eleven, ten, nine, eight, seven, six, five, four, three, two, and one. Now you come to see the colour purple for inspiration, indigo for expectation, aqua blue for communication, green for unconditional love, yellow for power and memory, orange for relationships, past lives and sexuality, and red for your *tribe* and moving forward with your life. Remember to say to yourself, "Every day in every way, my life gets better, better, and better."

By going within ourselves, we have a loving connection to the spirit world and with this help we are able to manifest and create our own reality in our minds so long as it is in accordance with our karma, comes with the highest integrity, and does not harm anyone.

WHAT ARE GUIDES
AND SPIRIT HELPERS?

Working with Guides

When we are born, we come in with our own guide and angel helpers. These loving spiritual beings are our main guides or gatekeepers to the soul who stay with us throughout our lives until we die. As we develop spiritually, lifting our vibrations, we bring in other guides who teach us what we need to know. I have between six to eight guides who come in and out of my life, but there are three who are always helping me with my work as a professional medium, teacher, and writer.

When I trance channel, I am protected by my main guide, an Indian entity called White Feather (who was once my father in one of my Indian lifetimes). This gentle soul is what I call the gatekeeper, and his duty is to make sure unwanted or malevolent spirits do not come into my energy field or cause me any harm.

Over the years he has moved to the side, and I now work mainly with a very wise and powerful guide called Romanov, who helps me with my stage shows and my work with the media. Before this guide came in, I had been suffering from headaches, but I have now seen that this was happening because there was a shift in my vibration, as the new guide was very powerful.

Often guides will come and go, and when we have finished working with them, they will step aside and allow another guide or guides with new vibration to come in to help with the spiritual journey and the progression of the soul. The guide that is our guardian is here to assist us with our everyday lives and our spiritual contract on Earth. When we have finished our time on Earth, our loving guide travels back with us once again to the spirit world. As the bond and love connection is so strong between the two, it could be understood that a past life may have been shared with this enlightened being.

Until we pass over to join our guides as spirits, they protect us from negative energies as they stay with us throughout our lives and protect our souls. When we nurture the bond between our guides and ourselves, the trust and natural relationship that develops can be of immense strength and may help us through more challenging times.

We may also have many guides throughout our lives and angels that come and watch over us. As we develop, different guides will come in, work with us, and leave. Over the years I have had many guides and know at least seven that have worked with me. As I have practiced trance mediumship for many years, I know who these guides are and what they can help me with. I decided to sit in a trance group to learn exactly who these guides were. There are many stages of trance mediumship, but mine is not the deep trance state, as I like to remember things. To know more about your team spirit guides, you need to sit in a spiritual development circle, and over time you will become very proficient. To learn more about my own guides and how they helped me, you can read my second book, *Memoirs of a Suburban Medium*, which can be bought as an e-book on Amazon.

Angels are another type of spiritual helpers. I have seen them when I work with past-life regression, as they often come in when people have experienced a tragic death in a past life. They are magnificent beings, but we need to call them in, as they only come around when we need them and when we ask for help. It is important when working with this high energy vibration to thank them for their assistance.

Working with Energy

When people ask me what I do for a career, I will often just tell them I am an energy worker. This seems to work better for me. Not only is it true, but it deters all the small-minded people who still live in the dark ages and who think mediums and healers are charlatans or witches of some degree. This became quite evident to me when I first opened my office not far from where I live. The real estate agent who leased me the property was quite happy to hear from his sister and mother in the spirit world but warned me not to call myself a psychic medium on my sign out in front, as it would upset the small village where we lived and the Christians who live in it.

Everything in the universe, including the planet and ourselves, is made up of and transmutes pure energy. We are like small transmitters sending out signals to others who have the same frequency or vibration as us and who will be attracted to our own energy. If you are a person who is happy and contented with your life, you will attract others who are the same and will want to help you. If, on the other hand, you are negative, nasty, or vindictive, you will always seem to draw bad experiences or negative energy towards you.

There are also two types of energy we can work with.

Light energy is loving, warm, and composed of unconditional love. This energy is stronger, healing, protective, and connected to the *Christ consciousness energy*, which is the most powerful and strongest energy in the universe.

Dark energy is thicker and extremely manipulative, works faster, but is extremely malevolent and, in most cases, has repercussions. For example, people who work with the dark arts, or this type of evil energy, may be successful for a while when they use it but in the long term they will suffer emotionally and will never feel fully loved in their personal relationships. The negative energy that they are working with will always, without question, bounce back to them according to the universal laws. As the saying goes, what you throw to others will always be returned. Often when I am clearing dark energy from clients, their homes, land, or business premises by burning sage or dried gum leaves, I will find this energy hard to work with. With time and patience it will eventually go into the column or portal of light I have brought down from the spirit world.

For any leftover energy that does not want to cross over, I will call on my guide and angel helpers to help me release it back into Mother Nature, in the ground. With the help of the elemental kingdom I am able to send it back into the earth for healing, as I know it will not transmute back into the light. The type of negative energy I am talking about is not nice, and you really do not want to know about it, as it is often associated with murders, assaults, and indecent acts that have occurred in that vicinity.

Protection

All matter has an energy field, what we call an aura. To heal or improve our own energy we can use different methods. These include talking a walk in nature, swimming in the sea (saltwater cleanses the aura), listening to music (which can be very uplifting), meditating, and doing grounding exercise (walking, martial arts, or going to the gym), and we can also use a good healthy diet to raise our energy when we are feeling depleted.

It is also wise to keep away from negative people who drain your energy or want things from you all the time.

As you work more on yourself and meditate on a daily basis, you not only lift your vibration or energy but also become more sensitive. As a result, you need to protect yourself more from other people's negative energies or frequencies, as they may drain you or affect you in some way.

We are all made up of energies or frequencies, and we all send out all types of energy with our thought forms like transmission stations or telegraph poles. Earth is like a large interesting stage where we play out our lessons. As part of our development as souls, we are here to learn as part of our spiritual contract here on earth. Once this happens, so-called friends or acquaintances may also leave your life, as they are no longer part of your spiritual contract.

People you attract or people who are in your life are drawn to your energy. Anyone who hurts you in any way, i.e. family members, friends, lovers, or acquaintances, is what is called a spiritual lesson. Once you have learnt the lesson, you need to forgive them, send them love, and move on past the karma. Otherwise we may lose our power and become stuck, angry and confused. No matter how much we may think we love them (often from past lives), people who are not in our lives are not meant to be there. They have their own karma and learning to complete elsewhere.

Case Study

Karen met David at a meditation group. From the first moment their eyes met, they both felt a deep spiritual connection that was very intense and confusing. They were drawn to each other and wanted to spend more and more time together. Karen, who was quite a bit older than David, was already married with children and still loved her husband. Looking to get clarity on her situation, she came to me for a past-life regression. When she did this, she saw (as she suspected) that she and this other man had lived many past lives together, one as a married couple, another as brother and sister, one as good friends, and even one as mother and child.

At the end of the session her own guide came in and told her that they were not meant to be together in this lifetime, as they had their own spiritual contracts and work that was taking them in different directions. No matter how hard they tried to fight against their destinies, they were finally torn apart by the powers that be and ended up living in different states. Not long after Karen opened her heart up to her husband again and moved on with her important spiritual work as did David with his. They still stay in contact but from a great distance, as love is eternal, but both were happy to move on and do the work they were meant to do.

Contract Player

David was just one of Karen's soul mates. We can have up to seven in a lifetime. We don't necessarily meet them all in one lifetime, but often they will come in as catalysts to help us move along our path. David's role in this lifetime was not to be with Karen again, but he had made a spiritual contract to help her move on with the personal problems she was having in her marriage with her husband. By entering her life again, he was awakening her to her own love of the goddess within and her divine inner beauty.

Sometimes our lives can become very busy as we get caught up in the humdrum of life. Sadly when this happens, we forget to love ourselves and the people who mean the most to us. When this happens, we will often have what I call an insight or spiritual awakening from people who suddenly come into our lives to wake us up and then move on. These people are what I call contract players. They come from our own soul groups in the spirit world or the soul groups around us to wake us up. We may not understand what is going on at the time and may be confused for a while, but on reflection and with time we will see what this encounter really meant.

How to Protect Yourself

1) Always bring down white light energy for protection and run it all around you as a protective barrier or shield. You can also do this to your loved ones as well as your home and possessions. If you are having a really hard time, as extra protection try using gold light as well. Just imagine, in your mind's eye, the energy as the sun and wrap it around your body and aura, dissolving any darkness or shadows.

2) Exercise strong boundaries with everyone in your life. Always listen to your intuition. It is never wrong, as it is often your higher self or soul energy talking to you, or it might be your guide stepping in as well. I don't know how many times I have heard people say to me that they had a feeling something was wrong or that a thought telling them something went through their heads. These moments of truth, gut feelings, and knowing are real and should be listened to. Sometimes the subconscious mind will show us the answers to problems in our dreams.

3) Make sure you eat a balanced diet. Everything should be taken in moderation, and that includes alcohol.

4) When you are feeling drained of energy, have a good soak for at least twenty minutes in a salt bath with a handful of Epson salts. This will clear away any negative energy and debris you many have collected in your aura or energy field. Waving a smoking sage stick through your aura will do the same.

5) Cloaking is another way to protect yourself. If you do not want to be noticed when you are walking into a room or when you are out and about, pull your aura in and imagine you have on an invisible cloak that wraps around you. This will pull in your energy, and you will be able to walk around and mix with people without them paying you too much attention.

6) Another way of clearing negative energy is by smoking yourself all over with some dried sage.

7) Playing music, drumming, or playing an instrument can be very uplifting.

8) Meditating for at least twenty minutes a day and making positive affirmations are an energy boost. Make it a rule to close down all your chakras or energy points after you work with people or meditate. This is a good way to protect yourself so you are not *open* to other people's energy or vibrations.

9) Having a good laugh and catch up with some good friends.

10) Grounding exercises (walking, martial arts, going to the gym, or dancing, doing yoga, or exercising) help to raise your energy and will prevent you from feeling depleted. Exercise, a healthy diet, and taking care of yourself will get you grounded. A lot

of students I have worked with over the years have had this problem. When they are not grounded to the Earth, they are very scattered and not able to grow spiritually and reach their higher powers.

11) Make time for fun with friends and loved ones.

12) Have healthy boundaries. Don't feel depleted by too many people taking your energy. Set goals and see how fast you can manifest them.

13) Get rid of people that are draining and negative. You will find they are just sucking your energy and wasting your time. I can't stress enough how important this is because you need to have good friends as well, not just people in your life you feel you need to help all the time.

14) Learn to say NO. It feels good, as it is a powerful thing to be able to do and boundaries are a healthy practice to have.

15) Lose the clutter in your home. Anything that does not serve you is just blocking the energy.

16) Most importantly, learn to love yourself. If you don't, nobody else will. Be willing to forgive loved ones, people, or friends who have hurt you in some way. This can be really hard, as these painful lessons can take you off your path, disempower you, and hold you back from where you are meant to be. It may be sad in some cases not to have them in your life again, but if they are meant to come back and are the right energy for you, they will return when they have completed their own lessons. An easy way to do this is to simply place them in a large pink healing bubble of love, tell them that you forgive them, and let them go, surrendering your pain to the spirit world.

Clearing Negative Energy

To clear any type of space, always use sage (*grandfather* or white sage is the best) or dried gum leaves and white light to *sweep* yourself, your client, or your place of work. This will clear away any toxic or negative energy that may have accumulated. This method is also excellent to get rid of lost souls that are stuck in the astral and have not crossed into the spirit world. The sweeping weakens them and encourages them either to pass over to the other side or simply depart from the space they have inhabited.

To do this, place some grandfather sage or dried Australian gum leaves in a round bowl (one that does not get used for cooking anymore) and light the leaves until they start to burn and produce a smoky effect. Take your time and slowly walk through the areas you want to clean, making sure you smoke the corners of the room as well as cupboards, filling each room with this powerful, pungent smoke. Make sure all the windows in the home are closed to get maximum effect. Once you have finished smoking all your spaces, wait about ten minutes until the smoke has settled and then open all windows so it can escape out. This in turn will eradicate any negative energy and make earthbound spirits want to leave quick smart. Once the room is aired, you will feel the difference, as everything will feel and appear clearer and lighter.

Essential oils, such as sandalwood, frankincense, lavender, rose, pine, juniper berry, and myrrh, are wonderful for clearing out old energy and cleaning the aura. They all have a very relaxing effect and calm the senses. Cedar wood is soothing and uplifting, and it replaces negativity with optimism. Cypress mixed with lemon and geranium is very healing and cleansing as well. Using thyme, sage, peppermint, and rosemary brings in love energy and enhances mental powers. Lavender is very calming and helps relax and soothe the nerves and the senses.

Grounding Yourself

It is important to stay grounded, healthy, and focused when you are doing this work, as it comes with an enormous amount of energy and responsibility that most people are not aware of. People, who are not grounded, may have emotional problems or addictions and are usually not in their own bodies so are not able to give positive and loving messages. Not only are you working as a clear channel, connecting to your client's guides, loved ones, and spirit helpers, but you are often called on to be a wise counselor for clients who are often lost and having so many problems.

On a personal level I worked as a trained nurse for many years and saw death on a daily basis. Through this often traumatic experience, I was able to learn good counseling skills, which I use every day. It goes without saying that anyone who wants to do this work should have some type of counseling, grief, and bereavement skills. Once you are on this path, spirit will send you all types of people from all walks of life, people who will be attracted to your energy like a magnet and will need your assistance and help in many ways. Make sure you keep your boundaries up and your protection intact and do not take these people on as friends, as often you are just there only for them and they will drain you of your own energy.

Many times I have walked into a shop and someone, either working there or just shopping, will just come up to me and tell me all their problems. I have also worked in the media where other so-called readers, healers, and other mediums have suddenly befriended me just so I can help them in whatever is going on in their lives. Once they receive the information they need, they will move on, and your kindness is often never reciprocated for the fantastic so-called *swap* they were going to give you.

Psychic attack was another problem I encountered when I first opened up, and I must have been an easy target for so many parasites out there in the astral. Meditation helped with this, as it lifted my energy and increased my vibration, allowing increased light into my light body until the dark forces, parasites, and other entities found it almost impossible to affect me in any way. Daily exercise help keeps you strong and fit both mentally and physically. Practicing a martial art is an excellent way to keep your energy grounded, focused, and in alignment, especially if you are very sensitive and psychic because you will be able to work for long hours and stay focused. These days there are so many ways to stay fit and healthy, such as chakra dancing or any exercise you can have fun with.

A well-balanced, healthy diet full of protein and essential carbohydrates with plenty of fresh water, organic vegetables, and fruits is also encouraged when you do any type of spiritual work. Often people who do not eat properly, indulge in rich, fatty foods or recreational drugs, and consume large amounts of alcohol are not very focused, and their energies are what I call "all over the place."

I once worked with a woman who was a very good reader until she started to drink every night because of her personal worries and emotional problems, which she never seemed to deal with over the years. After a while her readings became extremely negative and off the mark, and it was no surprise when her clients suddenly dropped off like flies until she was forced to close up her business.

Another extremely ambitious woman I worked with in the media starved herself on a daily basis so she could look a certain way. I know the camera does add to our frames, but her obsession with herself and what she looked like went way beyond the extreme. In the end she was totally scattered, and her readings never made any sense at all. Before too long she became very sick, forgot what shifts she was supposed to work, and was no longer looked upon as a reliable worker. It was not too long after that she was asked to leave and was replaced by another medium.

I have always believed that healthy food breeds a healthy mind and healthy body. If we could just remember our bodies are our temples to use in this life. We need to take care of them. We could perform so much better at work and reach the top of our fields if only we paid attention to the type of food we put in our mouths.

The more you work on yourself, meditate daily, and refrain from negative excesses, the more *light* you will bring into your own light body. You will notice that a vegetarian diet is a good thing, but your mind has to be stress-free and happy as well. That is why meditation is so important in our lives. It will also *clear* your channel and give you a strong energy link to the spirit world, where you will have an excess of loving information given to you on a daily basis.

Vibrational flower essences, such as clematis in the Bach Flower Essences and red lily in the Australia Bush Flower Essences, are good for grounding when taken in a daily dose. If you feel ungrounded, a good way to clear your head is to go out in nature. Stand barefoot on the grass or soil, raise your hands above your head while you are breathing in, and extend your fingers, slowly lowering them towards the Earth while breathing out. Also just the simple act of hugging a tree will ground you.

Ever since I started doing this work professionally, which is part of my spiritual purpose or contract; I have always meditated and made an effort to exercise every day. This has become an integral part of my work. This process not only keeps me strong physically, mentally, emotionally, and spiritually but also helps keep my channel clear. I am able to raise my vibration to a higher level and access information needed for my clients. I also love cycling, spin classes, bushwalking, and surfing in the sea. When I was younger, I would spend hours with my little board in the waves, but these days I concentrate more on lap swimming to strengthen my core. Listening to music, catching up with friends, and other entertainment add some fun and it can help make your life a little less serious and balanced.

Thought Forms

It is important to monitor your thought forms all the time. Have you ever heard the saying, "What you believe you become"? Learn to surround yourself with only positive loving people and always listen to *positive* thought forms only. Also be aware of negative patterns in your life and mind. We create our own reality, so why not make it as positive and beautiful as possible? What's wrong with creating a beautiful heaven on earth? Negative, abusive people only take or steal away our energy if we let them and take us down a heavy, tiring path, leading us astray from our true spiritual purpose. Stay away from the self-pity of the world, as it can be draining as well and these individuals are really *energy stealers.*

Sometimes a negative thought form can build up in the aura, making us feel unhappy with ourselves. You can see this if you view the aura, as it will look very dense and appear above the crown chakra as a thick, dirty brown colour. We can also build up negative thought forms, thinking we are unworthy of long-term relationships for example. In turn, if this is not dealt with, it will become part of a negative belief structure. To deal with this, visualize a beautiful pink bubble above your head and place all your negativity into it. When it is full, simply surrender it to God and let it go.

Years ago I sat in a meditation group with an older lady who had suffered from cancer and had both breasts removed. Her doctor understood her fear of the disease returning again and suggested she change her mind-set by putting all her problems of the day into a *Jesus* bottle she had beside her bed. Every night before she went to sleep, she would write all her frustrations, worries, and anxieties down on a piece of paper and lovingly slip it into the little bottle. She often told us about this when we would meet, and we would all have a good laugh. As far as she was concerned, she was finished with cancer and truly believed it would never come back, as her Jesus bottle took care of all her worries.

Forgiveness and unconditional love is the key to all healing. Always be willing to forgive loved ones, people, or friends who have hurt you in some way. An easy way to do this is to simply place them in a big pink healing bubble of love, tell them that you forgive them, and let them go, surrendering your pain to the spirit world.

The Four Clairs

Discovering Your Communication Form

Every person has four methods or channels for receiving divine guidance through sight, sound, feelings, and thought. People newly on the spiritual path usually have only one or two channels opened at first. With meditation for just twenty minutes a day done with dedication to your work and spirit, your abilities will increase tenfold. Just as you give love to something, you will always see growth.

Over time you will be delighted because you will find your gifts will improve and you will look back and see just how far you have come. Spirit will never give you anything you cannot handle, but if this does seem to happen with a premonition in a dream that scares you for example, ask the spirit world to take it away until you are ready.

Clairvoyance or Clear Seeing

Clear seeing brings divine guidance as still pictures or miniature movies in or outside your head. When I younger, I used to see pictures in my mind's eye of people who looked like other people. This was my intuition telling me that the person I was seeing really wasn't who they said they were. Also when I am reading for clients, spirit will often give me a full picture or a small movie of what they want the relatives to remember or know. As I am working constantly with spirit for clients, this ability is always improving and gives me a clear picture or indication of what is going on in the people's lives, as the spirit world will always show one past, present, and future.

Clairvoyance Exercise 1

This is a great exercise to do when you want to open up and work with your third eye and use your clairvoyance abilities. Begin with understanding that your third eye is like a muscle. The more you work with it, the better it will become for you in your spiritual work over time. You will begin to see little pictures in your mind's eye, and spirit will show you things like visions and pictures, which is a wonderful ability to have. To begin, give your third eye a small workout by squeezing the area or muscle by opening and closing it—squeezing open, squeezing close. Do this a few times before you begin the next exercise.

Clairvoyance Exercise 2

1) Sit in a comfortable position in your sacred space. Taking a few deep breaths in and out. Feel your whole body slowly relaxing.

2) Gently close your eyes and feel yourself relaxing even more. Next feel yourself opening up all your chakras one by one, ending with the Earth star chakra, which is situated in the ground. Then imagine yourself sitting at the back of your third eye. No matter what happens, pay special attention and give full concentration to this exercise.

3) Look for any pictures that may float through your mind's eye but just notice them. These are simply things that are on your mind, just like you are sitting in a room, and are usually clutter from the day or about others who may need your attention. If this is the case, let them go and deal with them later.

4) When you have finished this exercise or any spiritual exercise and even mediation, remember to close your energy down by imagining all your chakras like little lights all turning off. Then remember to use your protection by wrapping a beautiful white energy all around yourself and under your feet and using a soft golden light like the sun all around your body.

Clairaudience or Clear Hearing

For me this ability has improved with age and has been very beneficial when I am doing psychic shows or on the platform at spiritual churches, as it gives me a direct link to spirit in my mediumship. Often when I am working with a large audience, I will hear names being called out from the spirit world, names of those who have passed over. This helps me to connect to someone in the audience whom the spirit wishes to contact with a message.

Clairaudience Exercises

1) Learn to listen to the stillness. Each day count how many sounds you can hear. Take a walk in nature and learn to listen to the earth, trees, plants, and insects. Sit by the water and listen to the wind and the waves or ripples.

2) Learn to hear the birds and everything in nature that is around you. Every living thing has a blueprint and an energy you can hear.

3) Practice remembering the sounds of songs and the sound of your family and friends and also sing vowels to clear the throat chakra.

4) Clear your ear chakras out by calling in clear, white light. They are located next to your own ears. Imagine you have a dial inside your ear chakras that can be turned up when you want to hear spirit.

5) Release any doubts or fears you have about hearing into the light.

6) Close down (as discussed before).

CLAIRCOGNISANCE OR CLEAR KNOWING

This simply means clear knowing without any doubt about how you know.

Claircognisance takes many forms.

1. Revelations: Having a profound revelation that you are one with the angels and God, that you are in the right place at the right time, or that something is just meant to be.

2. Aptitudes: Knowing how to fix or do something without even knowing how you know how to do it.

3. Facts: Somebody asks you something, and you seem to know everything about it without even knowing how you know this information.

4. Insights: For some reason you know the core issue of a problem without even knowing much about the situation.

5. Inspiration: You find yourself writing or saying ideas and concepts that you had never thought about before.

6. Ingenuity: You have an idea about a new invention that is time-saving, life-saving, or otherwise vitally needed in the world.

7. Foresight: As you are introduced to a new person or situation, you know exactly what the future course of this relationship or situation will be.

8. Faith: Ask God and the angels to take away any fears you have about trusting your gift of pure divine guidance. Always have faith.

Clairsentience or Clear feeling

This involves receiving divine guidance as an emotion or physical sensation, such as a smell, tightened muscles, or the sense of a touch. Many of us have this gift, as it is with us from birth, but some are better developed than others. I have seen some of the best mediums, healers, and psychics in the world use this gift. It is a beautiful one to master, as it operates with a direct link from our heart chakra. As a ghost buster, I have a very sensitive nose that is good for smelling spirits when I'm helping them cross over. The downside to this is I am open to many allergies, as my nose is oversensitive.

Talking to the Higher Self and Working with Our Guides

Sometimes in life we have problems communicating with our loved ones or people in general. We are often put in situations in our lives when it is just about impossible to have a civil conversation because of our blocks or emotions. Nobody is perfect, and we've all had times when our emotions rule our intelligence, making it impossible to bring closure to a relationship, get on with the boss or a colleague, or simply move out of a bad situation.

By talking telepathically to the person's higher self (which is your own soul energy), we can conquer this problem. It is an easy technique that really works. Just by trusting in yourself and talking to the person's higher self, you can bring healing to any situation. One day a client named Tina came to me in tears. She was most upset and told me that every day for the past two weeks she was being harassed on her mobile phone. Every time she would answer it, there would be silence on the other end.

The phone would ring repeatedly every day after 5:00 p.m., sometimes up to twenty times, but when she would answer it, the person on the other end would suddenly hang up, leaving her terrified. She was desperate, as she felt somebody was stalking her and her life was in danger. She found it hard to sleep at night and was too scared to be alone or even walk down the street. Her usually happy disposition had changed overnight to one of desperation, depression, and anxiety.

Connecting to my higher self, I intuitively felt the perpetrator was a woman. Sitting her down, we determined who this woman was. The person who came to mind was somebody she had briefly met at a party who had once been the girlfriend of Tina's current boyfriend. The woman was obviously full of jealousy and was taking her revenge out on my client in a nasty and terrible way. Realizing this woman was the stalker; Tina was shocked and could not understand how anyone could be so mean and hurtful. She was a very spiritual and nice person who would never want to hurt anyone in any way.

The ex-girlfriend was obviously hurting and in a need of a healing so she could move on with her life. Feeling more relaxed now, Tina gently closed her eyes, and we proceeded with the following higher-self healing, successfully setting up a dialogue between Tina's higher self and this woman. By the conclusion of the healing, Tina was feeling a lot better, and she received no more phone calls.

If you have ever had a problem with a loved one, friend, family member, lover, or animal, try this simple technique and bring peace, love, and light into your life. Know that with good intentions, miracles can happen.

Higher-Self Healing Meditation

1) Sit in a comfortable position, making sure you have switched off the telephone and will not be disturbed.

2) Slowly breathe in and out three times, relaxing as you let go of any stored emotions and negativity from your mind and body.

3) Feel your loving connection to the source and fill yourself with unconditional love and light. This will make you feel calm, warm, and secure.

4) Picture an image of a beautiful pink bubble in front of you. This is a healing bubble. Now put the person you would like to have a dialogue with inside the bubble and then step inside yourself.

5) Ask that person if you have permission to talk to his or her higher self. A simple yes or no is all you want. When you have the person's approval, continue. (If you don't, keep asking until you

do.) Begin the dialogue in a gentle and calm way, stating clearly and precisely in a loving tone exactly what you want to say. Listen for an answer and keep talking to the person until you have reached a conclusion. If there is no conclusion, try again and there may be a better outcome next time.

Remember that with good intentions nothing is impossible in life no matter how complex the situation may seem to be.

Tarot Reading Guide

Simple Rules for Working with Clients or the Public

If you always work with the highest of integrity, spirit will look after you. If you practice this, you will always have food on your table, a happy home, and loving people in your life. As a light worker and healer, you have an enormous responsibility to not only your client and the general public but also yourself. If you need help or feel overwhelmed, out of your depth, or not able to help a client, always send him or her to a professional for help.

On a practical level being a member of a professional association will often prove to be a good channel for work, as you will probably be able to be listed on their website. You may also want to take out business insurance. Look for one that can encompass all areas of your business or businesses (if you have more than one income stream).

When I'm not using my cards, I always wrap them in a dark cloth and put them in a safe place so others cannot handle them in any way. I have three sets of tarot cards: one for myself, one for clients, and one for students.

This is the routine I recommend for conducting a tarot card reading.

- After you have opened yourself up, connected to your guide and are set to read for the day, always wash yourself and your cards with white light as if to sweep away any energy that has built up on the cards from other clients. The same goes for when you are finishing a reading. Close down, sweep yourself, and clear the energy from the cards before you move on to reading for the next person.

- You can do this with by using a rose quartz or amethyst crystal. Simply place it on your third eye and ask it to clear your cards at all times.

- In a reading *never* predict death, as you are not God. My rule is not to say negative things in a reading, as the last thing clients want is more negativity in their lives. Remember that they are coming to you for clarity and guidance. This is not your call, and after all, only spirit and God can predict someone's death.

- Remember when you are not using cards, wrap them in a dark-colored silk scarf or put them in a box to protect them so they do not collect unwanted energy.

- If you are not well or suffering from some emotional trauma, do not read cards, as often these vibrations can be projected into your client's reading.

- Major arcana are God's destiny or karma cards and there are twenty-two of these cards in a deck. You can't change the fate or outcome of a major arcana cards, as they represent spiritual contracts or lessons we have already signed up for in the spirit world. With minor arcana cards you can change the outcome by having a positive outcome. For example, you may pull the Nine of Swords, which may mean a worrying time is coming, but remember that a warning is always helpful to give you time not to react and keep a positive outcome. This in turn will help you handle the situation better.

- Never discuss clients with another person, as you have a contract of trust with your clients.

- Do not ring up the clients and ask them if they want more readings. If they want to get in contact, then give them a business card, but leave it up to their own discretion. All good mediums and healers are always busy because of their reputation. I have been working for many years now in the profession, and I have never really had to advertise my services, as I rely a lot on word of mouth. I once worked with a young woman who would ask for the client's phone number. But when she did so, often the client would be offended and not want to come back into the shop again for fear of running into the overzealous young woman who was just coming from *ego*.

- Never try to diagnose a medical condition, as you are not a trained physician. If you feel your clients need help in other areas, remember to move them on to a professional. Whenever I spot what looks like a blockage in a client's body, I will always suggest he or she get a check-up from a trained doctor.

- Never demand money from people by saying you can get rid of curses and then threaten them by saying their lives will be one disaster after the next (especially in love) if you don't help them. I have seen this too many times for my liking. Scoundrels demanding exorbitant amounts of money by promising that they can release curses sound very suspicious to me. I have heard of cases where one woman when she was holidaying in the United States was told that she would never meet her soul mate if she did not hand over a thousand dollars. The poor girl went on to believe this and is still single as we speak. No amount of healing or telling her otherwise seemed to help; as she was the convinced the nasty gypsy or charlatan knew better.

- I never use reversed cards in my readings, as I am not interested in telling my clients anything negative. Always be positive, as we are aiming for a healing with love and guidance from the angels.

THE TAROT CARDS

There are seventy-eight playing cards in a tarot pack, comprising twenty-two major arcana cards and fifty-six minor or lesser arcana in four suits of fourteen cards each. These suits are wands, cups, swords, and pentacles. Each minor card is numbered from one or ace to ten, except for the court cards, which are the page, knight, queen, and king.

Major Arcana Cards

These are what I call *destiny* or *karma cards*, which are aligned to where you are on your spiritual journey here on earth. These cards are powerful messages from the universe, as when they come up you must accept the fate of the cards and understand that their meaning is in divine alignment with the universe, where you are at this point in your life, part of your spiritual contract and where you are at with your own karma.

There are no so-called *bad* cards in the major or minor arcana (or minor cards). They are simply signposts of what is to come or what is around you at the time.

1) **The Fool (New Beginnings, Taking Chances)**

- New exciting beginnings; taking chances; entering a new chapter of your life with exciting possibilities as you step out into the unknown, without thinking and just taking chances.

- In No. 1 position—Naïve, but lands on their feet.
- In No. 10 position—New beginnings, new career.

When the Fool comes up in a spread, it means a new chapter of life with an exciting new phase is just about to begin. This is a blessing, as it is a wonderful time of new beginnings and new opportunities. It also gives us the chance to be open-minded and to have a positive attitude about the new developments that are about to present themselves in your life. However, a risk of some kind and a willingness to jump out into the unknown are required. You are now embarking on a new journey.

Case Study

Diana was a born psychic and medium who had a keen interest in the spiritual world for as long as she could remember. Unfortunately she never seemed to get anywhere in her life, as most of her time was spent caught up in family dramas and counseling friends that were always drawn to her for spiritual advice on their problems. This involved talking on the phone for hours on end, sitting with friends, and listening to all their problems while her own children were at school during the day.

When people told her she should be reading in a shop and being paid for her services, she shunned the idea because she was very shy. She had no confidence in herself and was scared she would not be good enough, which was not the case because she had already been helping people for years with her gifts.

One day a woman rang her out of the blue and asked her if she would come and read in her shop, as a friend had passed on her phone number. The woman said she was interested in giving Diana a trial, as she needed good card readers. When Diana asked her cards for some reflection on the matter, she pulled out the Fool card.

To Diana this was an indication that it would all work out. The card showed she had nothing to fear and just had to go with the offer that was presented to her. Once she started working for the woman in the shop, she soon became booked out and to her joy started getting work on a regular basis. This work soon led to other things the spirit world had planned for her, and before too long she was working for the police as a volunteer and had started her own radio show, which became very popular. She now travels overseas and is well known and respected in the industry.

2) **The Magician (Talented, Clever, Gifted)**

- Represents someone who has potential and skills, usually very talented.
- Emphasizes a need to step into your own personal power.
- In No. 1 position—the person is very clever with abilities and gifts he or she hasn't utilized yet. Gifted, smart, intelligent.
- In No. 2 position—the person has the ability to make money or has skills to make money.
- In No. 6 position—Ability to do things with their health/fitness.

- In No. 10 position—Ability to use skills if they've just started a new job.

The Magician is a welcome card because it points to potential skills and creative abilities that have not yet manifested. This symbol may appear as an upsurge of energy and an intuition of exciting, new opportunities. The universe is now pulling out all the stops, as it supplies all the wisdom tools and insights in life. When the clever Magician appears, it becomes clear that the journey is possible and that there is new learning. It is important to be positive because the subject is now aware and has all the capacities he or she needs but are yet to be developed.

Case Study

Steve was a good friend of mine who was a male nurse and who ran an operating theatre for a large hospital. He was a natural-born leader when it came to delegating and organizing the other nurses and various doctors. Although very accomplished in his field of work, he was always studying. When I worked with him, it was not hard to see he was highly intelligent and well capable of coping with the stress and organizing of the busy surgical operating theatres. It was quite obvious to me that he had enormous potential to go to the top of any chosen field because of his interest and dedication to his chosen career.

When I did a reading for him one day over a cup of coffee, he came up as the Magician, and I encouraged him to keep working at his craft. He now runs one of the biggest operating theatres in the country and has worked all over the world in his chosen profession. He is a born leader, and his abilities coupled with the skills he is always learning enable him to handle any situation his work throws at him.

3) **The High Priestess (Highly Intuitive, Higher-Self Card)**

- Someone who is highly intuitive; the higher-self card.
- In No. 1 position—the person is very intuitive and needs to trust his or her intuition. They are sensitive. They need to trust their dreams. Journaling or writing things down will help.
- In No. 3 position—Friend or family member who is highly intuitive.
- In No. 9 position—Spiritual awakening; higher-self card; opening up to spirituality.

The appearance of the High Priestess in a spread is beautiful, as it represents the heightening of the powers of intuition like the opening of petals with a flower. This indicates an initiation or spiritual awakening and implies that there will be an encounter of some kind within the subconscious mind. The individual may be drawn inexplicably to this world through an interest in the occult or the esoteric or through the effects of a powerful dream or the uncanny sense that something is at work in his or her life. There may be confusion and bewilderment for a while, but he or she should trust in the process, as this always happens when one is opening up and going to another level on the spiritual path.

Case Study

Michelle was a bright, young woman who was a natural reader, healer, and psychic. But she was scared of her gift and did not often use it because when she did so it always got her into trouble. Being the black sheep of the family, her own family shunned her whenever she wanted to talk about the subject. They called her *weird* and *a dreamer* whenever she told them about her dreams or experiences.

I suggested she should not listen to their negativity and learn to trust her feelings. She needed to own her innate energy, which in reality was never wrong. I also encouraged to her to practice meditation once a day so she could form a friendship with her guides, who were there to help her on her spiritual journey. She took my advice and now runs a busy practice and has never looked back. She has also come to realize that when you work for spirit, it always looks after you. On the spiritual journey our study and work is always ongoing, as we never know it all.

4) **The Empress (Birth Card)**

- This is the birth card signifying success and bright prospects for new business ventures and lifestyle.
- Represents new beginnings.
- In No. 6 position—Pregnancy.
- In No. 4 position—New home, new beginnings in the home.
- In No. 10 position—New job or changes in career.

When the Empress card comes up in a spread, it suggests the onset of an earthier phase of life. A marriage or the birth of a child might occur, or the birth of a creative child or an artistic offspring may happen, for this, too, require the patience and nurturing of the Great Mother. Through this card we enter the realm of the body and the instincts as a place of both peace and stagnation, life-giving and life-suffocating.

Case Study

Often when I see the Empress card in a reading, it means a time of great abundance is coming into the client's life on many levels. It can also mean the birth of a child or pregnancy (if they're asking for themselves). One day a lovely Scottish woman named Mary came to me for a reading, wanting to know if the fertility treatment she was having was going to work. She had tried for years to get pregnant and was desperate to have children. She had spent a great deal of money on the treatments; however, unfortunately nothing had worked, and she was always disappointed.

When she came for the reading, I could see she had a few spirit children next to her in her aura. Then a spirit woman came through, who told me she was her grandmother and not to give up, as Mary would be having twins within the year. Mary was rendered speechless and started crying when I pulled out the Empress card, which clarified the whole situation. She was shocked not only with the good news but also about meeting her grandmother again, as she had died many years ago.

About one year later Mary rang me from overseas to say that her grandmother was right. She had gotten pregnant, and she was overjoyed to tell me that she had miraculously given birth to triplets. When she told me this, I did not know whether to laugh or cry. Be careful what you wish for.

5) **The Emperor (The Builder Card)**

- Male energy; a builder; earthy; building materialistic things.
- In No. 1 position—Strong; grounded; confident; go-getter; ambitious; someone who likes to make money; materialistic.
- In No. 6 position—Health is good; fixated on exercise.
- In No. 7 position—Solid marriage; materialistically doing okay.
- In No. 11 position—Social works.

We are often challenged to be successful in life or make something manifest, to realize a creative idea, to build something in the world, to found a business perhaps, or to establish the structure of a home and family. We are asked to take a standpoint, to become effective and powerful, or to formulate our ideas and ethics. We are also asked to consider where the creative young king has become the rigid, oppressive tyrant and where our ideologies are interfering with our lives and new growth.

Case Study

Adam was a very hard-working and ambitious young man who had just started a new business. He came to me for a reading, as he wanted to know whether he was going to be successful in his endeavors. He had worked very hard to get where he was in his new business venture. When I saw the Emperor card come up in the career section of the reading, I assured him he would have great success and not to worry. Within a few weeks of the reading I could see he would be signing a new contract that would take him overseas with his work. About six months later he rang me to say that it had all happened for him just as the cards had predicted. He was living the life he had dreamed of since he was young and was excited about all the positive events and constant travel.

6) **The Hierophant (Spiritual Teacher Card)**

- Have faith that everything will work out and unfold as it is meant to.
- In No. 1 position—Good teacher; teaching people things; quite a spiritual teacher in his or her own way.
- In No. 5 position—Teaching of lessons in relationships, love, and so on. Pull another card on it for more information. There is a lesson to be learned.

This card may emerge as the study of a particular philosophy or system of belief or as a deep commitment to a quest for meaning in life. It is asking the subject to surrender any worries or fears he or she may be having.

47

The Hierophant may appear in the form of an analyst, psychotherapist, priest, or spiritual mentor in outside life, someone whom the individual turns to for comfort and help.

Case Study

I first began to understand this card fully when I was going through a period of changes in my life. I was at the end of a career in acting that did not serve me any longer, as the parts I was getting were not what I wanted and only made me feel depressed and frustrated. It was as if all the doors were closing and my acting life, which I loved and had difficulty leaving after twenty-two years, was coming to an end. I could feel my life was changing in another way, taking me in a new direction. My guides had been telling me for months that I needed to work for spirit, which was my true calling.

When I kept pulling this card from my deck, I realized spirit was telling me that it was time to study, sit in a spiritual development group, and move on to other things. Before too long I enrolled in a hypnotherapy course, studied past-life regression, and learnt all about vibration therapies, such as Australian and Bush Flower essences. These all became part of my busy practice.

My mediumship, because of my dedication and my wonderful new teacher, soon began to draw more people into my life for readings, and my psychic abilities began to get stronger and stronger. I soon began to meditate on a daily basis, and a new door opened—one full of opportunity as my life changed dramatically. Once I made this decision, my main guide, White Feather, who is also my main teacher, stepped in, and I have never looked back.

7) The Lovers (Choice Card)

- Usually relates to love or job situation, with some emotion involved. Excellent results for love for singles. For married couples. Happy times are coming up for with a new lease of passion in the relationship.
- In No. 1 position—Dual personality; moody; problems with making decisions.
- In No. 2 position—Big spender; can't save; goes to extremes.

When this card appears in a spread, it means there is the need to make a choice of some kind, usually in love or career. The subject is asked to just follow what he or she feels, as this is the truth that will help in the decision and it will always result in a good outcome.

Case Study

Ruby was a client of mine who was engaged to her boyfriend of many years, a lovely, kind man named Bruce, and they were planning to marry. Everything was going well until Ruby started a new job and fell madly in love with her new boss, Paul, whom she claimed was her true soul mate after she had known him only for a couple of weeks. She loved Bruce very much, and they were good friends; however, her new relationship was life-changing, and it did not take long before her life was in chaos. She felt guilty about her feelings and did not know what to do.

When I did the reading, I could see Paul was already married and had no intention of leaving his wife and young family for her. But on the other hand, I told her how I saw him as a spiritual connection to show her that perhaps she was not really in love with her fiancée in the first place; especially if she was having such strong feelings for someone she had just met. Of course, they had past lives together, but this did not mean it was going to repeat itself again in this lifetime.

I told Ruby to think very hard about her decisions and not to just throw herself into a relationship where there would be only sorrow and frustration. After great deliberation she rang me six months later and told me she had left both men. She was living overseas to *sort her head out*; however, she still loved Bruce, and they were both willing to give it another go.

8) The Chariot (Eventual Success Card)

- The victory card. Struggle and suffer but success will result!
- Tenacious; nothing will stop them when it comes to career.
- Having a tough time with marriage or career, but they will be able to work through it.

The Chariot appearing in a spread will often mean conflict and struggle that can result in a stronger personality. The subject may come face-to-face not only with aggression in others but with his or her own competitive and aggressive drives. This conflict cannot be avoided but needs to be faced with strength and containment. Through this he or she will be able to grow and move forward with victory.

Case Study

Simon was happily married to his childhood sweetheart, Julia. They had been together for many years and also had two lovely children, a boy and a girl who became the focus of their lives. Things soon changed though when Simon, an artist, went to work in a nearby studio and fell madly in love with a woman who also worked there and did the same type of work as he did. Julia, who was pregnant at the time with her third child, was overcome with grief. Everyone who knew them ostracized Simon for behaving so badly and taking up a new relationship with his new lover when his own wife was so heavily pregnant and needed him.

Everything went downhill for Simon after that, as all his friends and both families wanted nothing to do with him. He was branded a selfish, bad man and a pariah, and it did not take too long before everyone he once knew completely left his life. Devastated and almost broken, he came to me for a reading. Putting my own feelings aside because I knew them both, I was happy to see the Chariot card appear in the reading. I told him to just hang in there, as this was what he truly wanted. Although it would be a rough ride, everything would settle within two years to peace and harmony again, not with his wife but with his new lover. Ten years later Simon is now married to his lover, and they both have a successful art business.

9) **Justice (Brings Clarity and Balance into Life)**

- Weighing up the pros and cons.
- Bringing more balance into all areas of life.
- Learning to understand and honor their emotions.
- Peaceful times and harmonious outcomes to all conflicts they may be having in life.
- In No. 12 position—A need to bring balance into life; out of control.
- In No. 5 position—A need to bring balance into relationships.

The card of Justice appearing in a spread indicates the need for balanced thought and an impartial decision-making process.

Case Study

When Susan came to me for a reading, she was working two jobs and seeing several potential boyfriends. She was unable to make rational decisions, such as where she wanted to live, and she was staying with friends. Since she had returned from living overseas the previous year, her life had been like riding a fast train that never stopped. After I talked to her for a while and scanned her energy, I sensed her inability to make decisions and asked if I could clear the clutter compounded around her head and upper body. Once I had done this, she said that she sensed an enormous relief and that she had not felt so relaxed for a very long time.

I suggested she try a daily meditation to help clear her mind, focus her thoughts, and ground her, as her energy was all over the place, making her feel very scattered. By simply meditating and reflecting on herself as a soul, she would bring more harmony, balance, and order into her life.

10) **The Hermit (Withdrawal Card)**

- Going within; soul searching; looking for answers to find out who they are as a soul and their spiritual purpose. This will take them to a higher vibration energetically, and life will be easier.
- In No. 7 position—Marriage; ask if they feel alone? Have they tried to communicate with their partner or get counseling?
- In No. 10 position—do they get any support at work?
- In No. 11 position—Person is a loner.

When the Hermit card comes up, it means there will come a time of growth and restlessness. It is saying that it is time to withdraw from everyday activities and go within to find the answers to the big questions they are seeking. It is a time for divine aloneness or withdrawal from the external activities of life so that the wisdom of patience may be acquired. There is an opportunity to build solid foundations with the higher self, guides, and angels if the subjects are willing to have perseverance and effort in meditation. Often when the Hermit card comes into a reading it is indicating the need to take time out to reflect on life. It can mean taking time out for themselves and honoring their own needs and wants, which can sometimes get squashed in the turmoil of everyday life.

Case Study

Mark came to me for a reading after he split with his wife of several years. It had been a difficult decision, as he did not want to hurt her. He was adamant he had made the right decision because in reality he had not wanted to marry her in the first place. He was fond of his wife, Kelly; however, he thought of her more like a good friend, and he always had the feeling she was not the *right one* but felt obligated to just go along with the marriage because of the expectations of family and friends.

The couple had never really had great *chemistry* or connection from the start, so it was not surprising it was impossible for Kelly to have children, something that Mark had always dreamed of. They would always argue, and Mark felt tired most of the time and ended up suffering from a serious health issue that affected every aspect of his life. As soon as the marriage was over, Mark decided to take time out to just reflect and try to find himself. This time for reflection on his so-called mistakes had a positive healing effect on him, and he was able to forgive Kelly and himself and move on with his life.

11) **The Wheel Of Fortune (Big Unforeseen but Positive Changes)**

- Welcome card—unforeseen changes, usually good.
- In No. 6 position—Changes in health, new health kick.
- In No. 10 position—Big changes in career.

The Wheel of Fortune means a sudden change of fortune. Finally destiny and good karma are working and bringing great joy and harmony with hopes, dreams, and wishes. This is a positive turn of events, as the Wheel brings growth and a new phase into the subject's life.

Case Study

Lauren was a client of mine who came for a reading. She was in stuck in her life, needed direction, and wanted change, as she was so unhappy. Like me, she had trained as an actress for many years but was unable to get any work in this area. She felt depressed. All her dreams and hopes of making it in her chosen profession were futile because she was rejected at every audition. To make ends meet she had been working as a checkout girl in a busy supermarket and hated her job with a passion. As she sat opposite me, crying softly into a tissue, it was easy to feel and see her sadness. However, I could not help but feel confused, as her cards were telling me another story.

As soon as I spread the cards out on the table, I saw the Wheel of Fortune come up in her spread, telling me her life was about to change for the better. Within three months there would be travel with a theatre company that would take her all over the world. When I told her this, she nearly fell off the chair, as she had just auditioned for a company that travelled overseas. Apparently they liked her work but said they had given the job to somebody else. Smiling, I reassured her again and said there was definitely travel and work with a theatre company coming up and she just had to have faith and wait and see.

A couple of weeks later she rang me again. This time it almost did not seem like the same person, as she was breathless, giggly, and overcome with emotion. The theatre company she auditioned for had asked her to come in again, and after the second audition, she was given the job. She had signed a contract with the company and would be travelling to Europe on tour within three months just as the cards had predicted.

12) **Strength (Strong Mentally, Physically, and Emotionally)**

- In No. 1 position—Strong person who has all the wisdom and strength they need.
- In No. 6 position—Health is good and strong.
- In No. 8 position—Good period.
- In No. 10 position—Career is good; nothing to worry about.

The Strength card, when it appears in a spread, is a good card because it is telling you all is well. It signifies a time to have the courage, strength, and self-discipline necessary to battle with the situation.

Case Study

This was another card that came up for me years ago when I realized I would no longer have any chance of making it in the acting profession. Since I was small, it had always been my dream to be a thespian, as I loved playing all the different character roles. I found it easier to do this than to simply be myself. I had already worked for a travelling theatre company, and I had worked extensively in film and television as an actress. But I soon realized that there were only so many jobs for so many people in that industry and that I unfortunately was not one of them.

When all the work had dried up, I had to sadly give up my failing acting career and get what my husband could only say was a *real job* with a steady income and money to pay the bills. Feeling extremely depressed and sad, I pulled the Strength card, which surprised me because I had thought my days on the stage were well and truly over. Little did I know that spirit had something else lined up for me years later. If it wasn't for my years of training as an actor, I would certainly not have had the courage and experience to do the real work with my spiritual abilities and my natural gift of mediumship.

Through my early training in the acting world, I have been able to find steady work writing and publishing books of a spiritual nature, perform easily on stage by delivering spirit messages to loved ones, and work extensively with the media. Often we do not see what spirit has planned for us in the future or the bigger picture on our life path.

13) **Hanged Man (Sacrifices Card)**

- This is time held in suspension and surrender, when there is a need to reflect and look at things from a different perspective.
- This also means a change for the better as we let go of any fears or negativity, surrendering it all to the universe to look after.

When the Hanged Man appears, it is time to surrender to whatever is going on in your life. It can also mean the need to make a voluntary sacrifice for the purpose of acquiring something of greater value. This might be the sacrifice of an external thing that has previously provided security. Hopefully some potential can be given room to develop. Or it can be the sacrifice of a cherished attitude, such as intellectual superiority or unforgiving hatred or a stubborn pursuit of some unattainable fantasy that is not going to work anyway in the way you may see it.

Case Study

No matter how hard Karen tried, she could never seem to meet the man of her dreams. She was always attracted to men with certain addictions or commitment problems. When she was younger, she was abused as a child, and she had therapy, but her personal relationships had suffered for years. When she came to me, she was thirty-nine years of age and feeling depressed about her life and what fate had given her. She was desperate to meet a good man and settle down but was too scared to make the move to go and meet people because of her terrible relationships in the past.

After I reviewed one of her past lives, which gave her a spiritual healing and took her to another level and vibration, we had a look at the cards. The Hanged Man came up in her relationship section along with the Ace of Cups, which indicated she would meet someone within the next six months.

14) **Death (Endings that Bring Exciting New Beginnings)**

- Finishing with the old; new and often better beginnings to come.
- In with the new and out with the old; don't be afraid of letting go!
- The finishing of a cycle in your journey of life.
- This is not a physical death but usually a sudden and dramatic change of circumstance. This is a time of transformation, total cleansing, and letting go of the old to bring in the new energy; planting the seed of new things to come and grow.
- In No. 1 position—Person is about to undergo a total transformation.
- In No. 5 position—Relationships finishing but new ones starting.
- If you get the Death and Tower cards together, then pull another card for a more accurate reading.

When the Death card comes up in a reading or spread, it is saying that something that no longer serves the subject must come to an end. Whether or not this experience is painful depends upon the person's capacity to accept and recognize the necessity of an ending. It is a sometimes sad but ultimately welcome card because it is also an opportunity for a new life if the person can let go of the old one.

Case Study

When people see the Death card, they often think of gloom and doom, but this is far from the case. This card has come up for me many times in my life when I am at the end of a relationship or career. It is what I call a welcoming card, as it is the beginning of a new phase, that can sometimes exciting but challenging at the same time. Often we just know or have a feeling that our angels are telling us that we are at the end of a phase in our lives and we will soon be heading in a new direction.

This card has come up for me many times in my life, and with sadness I always know I must move on but with the knowledge that new things are on the horizon. When one door closes, another always opens, no matter how hard or unlikely it may seem at the time.

I once dreamed my close girlfriend had died, and I felt so sad at the time. When I rang her the next day, she told me she had decided to move interstate and live with her boyfriend. I was happy for her, of course, but sad that she was moving away and would not be part of my life again, as we were like soul sisters and did everything together.

15) Temperance (A Time of Peace and Tranquility)

- A beautiful, gentle, soothing time in life.
- Finding solutions and balance in your life; a time of love and peace in relationships.
- Time of peace and tranquility.
- In No. 12 position—Coming into peaceful times.

The Temperance card in a spread implies the need for a flow of feeling in a relationship. It may also suggest the potential for harmony and cooperation, resulting in a good relationship or a happy marriage. We are challenged with the issue of learning to develop a balanced heart.

Case Study

Serena was a woman going through a difficult divorce. She had done well with her legal fight but was exhausted. When she came to me for a reading, her mother came through in spirit and said how proud she was of her daughter and of everything she had been through. She also said that she had been with her most of the time when she was going through difficulties. This was confirmed by my client, as she said she had *felt* her around her at that time.

As I laid out the cards, the first one that came out was the Temperance card, together with one that indicated a new man friend. When I told her this, she laughed and said it was the last thing on her mind. Her new man friend I had seen in the cards was called Michael, and they have been together ever since. Never underestimate the cards; they always know what is going to happen no matter what you may think!

16) The Devil Card (A Dark Side or Addictions)

- The person indicated could be dishonest, a constant worrier, someone who needs help; a need to curb bad habits or problems, such as mental illness, addictions, or depression.
- In No. 5 or No. 7 positions—Infidelity.
- In No. 10 position—This could be things going wrong at work.
- In No. 1 position—Mental illness, worrier, dishonesty, shady character.
- In No. 4 position—Something dishonest could be going on at home.

The Devil card always implies the need to confront the shadow side of the personality. It may also refer to problematic things or habits that include all types of addictions, negative thought forms, habitual worriers, and people who steal, lie, and cheat in any capacity.

Case Study

From an early age Marco was very bright and extremely creative and excelled at school with his studies. He was a shy boy, but life was difficult, as he was highly sensitive and suffered from depression. His one great happiness in life was writing his poetry and music, which he would spend hours working on, locked away in his room.

When he came to me for a reading, the Devil card came up, referring to his personality. When we discussed this, he told me he was on medication but sometimes found it hard, as it had side effects, making him not want to talk to people, as he would lock himself away and drink too much and then have no energy. Over the years we became kindred friends and ended up having a great connection as mates. We both had a love of music at the time, and I had the privilege of not only playing in his band but having a glimpse of his beautiful, sensitive mind, which was so full of lyrics and words and poetry.

When I look back and think of the times we had together, I realize spirit gave me an opportunity to work with of the most talented and gifted artists I have ever met in my life. Sadly Marco decided not to stay here, as it was all too hard, and he went to live in the spirit world. I will never forget our time together and the heartfelt joy our music gave us and so many that heard it. His beautiful lyrics will live on and stay in my heart and mind forever.

17) **The Tower (A Major Life Shake-Up!)**

- Put your seat belt on, as you are in for a rocky ride. Huge changes are coming up. You will survive!
- Everything around you crumbles for a reason, and there is an urgent need to reflect on your priorities. Remain calm and positive in this time of great change.
- In No. 7 position—Marriage is finished, no matter how hard you try to fix it.
- In No. 11 position—Lots of issues with friends coming up.
- If you get the Death and Tower cards together, pull another card for a more accurate reading.

When the Tower appears in a spread, know that the universe is saying the subject is on the wrong path and that his or her life is about to be turned inside out, as he or she is in an incredible time of learning. This card is the harbinger of change, as it is the total breaking down of existing familiar forms. The Tower card, like the Death and the Devil cards, depends a great deal upon the attitude of the individual in terms of how difficult or painful it is to deal with.

Obviously it is more responsible for the people to ask their inner selves where they might be constricted or bound by false personas or images because a willing effort to break through this pretence can spare a great deal of anguish.

But it seems that the Tower will fall anyway, no matter what they do, not because some malicious external fate decrees it but because something within has reached boiling point and it can no longer live within such confines.

Case Study

Years ago I was a budding young actress. It was always my dream to be a performer with music or as an actress on the stage, theatre, and films. As a child I was always play acting to fit in, performing and dressing up as various characters, and talking in different accents. My mother thought I was quite mad and said I had found my calling, as I was always the drama queen.

After studying for years with so much love and dedication, everything went along really well, and I ended up working as an actress and travelling all over the place. Suddenly everything changed. The contract I had with the company soon came to an end because of external circumstances. Heartbroken, no matter how I tried to get other work, all the doors were tightly closed. I got a few roles on television and did a few meaningless advertisements, but my heart was not in it.

My life as I knew it had come to an abrupt end, and there was a new path I was not seeing on the horizon. When I ended up at the doctor's surgery, suffering from depression and acute anxiety, and I was given a script for tranquilizers. To me this was a signpost to just sadly surrender all my own childhood dreams and see what fate had in store for me.

Later on reflection, when I gave myself a reading with my own tarot cards, I saw I had pulled out the Tower card, which was right on top of me. Automatically everything made sense, even though I felt angry thinking everything was so unfair, as the cards were showing me that it was my destiny to just let go and go in another direction.

As I surrendered my dreams to spirit, my life ended up going in a much better direction than I had ever expected, and I have never been happier. You may not know it, but there is always a better world out there.

18) **The Star (Hopes and Dreams Coming True)**

- This is a positive card. Be extremely optimistic and have faith. All hopes, dreams, and heartfelt wishes are coming true.
- Yes, you are going in the right direction, and your goals and dreams are within reach.
- You're a beautiful shining light to many around you.
- Positivity, hope, blessings, grace, and faith.
- In No. 1 position—Person lands on his or her feet; spiritual and talented, he or she shines in the world; people are attracted to this person. He or she is the *star* of his or her own show.

When the Star appears in a spread, it is a time to believe in your dreams as the subject experiences hope, meaning, and faith in the midst of personal difficulties. It is my favorite card in the tarot pack, as it is a beacon of light in perhaps troubled times and it gives a blessing of promise at a time when the individual may be down on his or her luck and losing faith in life and love. Stay positive, as life is on track and the subject will have the confidence and courage to reach all of his or her goals, dreams, wishes, and hopes. Be the star of your own stage of life and watch yourself prosper and glow.

Case Study

Michael had been married for many years to his wife, Bella, but after a difficult time and sadly no children, they both agreed they had grown apart and decided to split everything they had saved together and go their separate ways. Before too long Bella met someone else and moved in with him straight away. Poor Michael, although happy for her, if truth were told, also felt very sad because she had been able to move on before him and was even planning her next wedding.

When he came to me for a reading, he was feeling very sorry for himself. Before too long his late father came in the room in spirit and said Michael was not to worry, as he would be going to his own wedding soon and would soon be the father to a lovely child. Before he could say anything, I went on to tell him that he had also pulled the Star card in his relationship section of the spread. This new woman would be a soul-mate connection, and he would meet her within three months. For some reason he thought I had made it all up and stomped angrily out of my office when the reading was over. Six months later he rang me up, apologized, and said his late father was right. He had since met a lovely woman named Anna, who had never been married before and wanted a child with him.

19) **The Moon (Confusion Card)**

- If you have any decisions to make, it's not a good time to make them.
- Person is going through a major shift; time to go within.
- Spiritual transformation in life; getting rid of the old and in with the new.
- In No. 4 position—The person may have a cluttered house.
- Too much going on in their lives; can't focus on what's going on.

When the Moon appears in a spread, it usually means a period of confusion, fluctuation, and uncertainty. On a spiritual level it can also mean going to another level on the spiritual plane. Things may seem rocky for a while, so it is best to look after you and not make any big decisions. Your mind may be quite cluttered because you may be processing on a subconscious level.

Case Study

Rachel had wanted to have her own hair salon for many years. She was very hard-working person and independent until she met her boyfriend, Ricky, who was always in and out of jail. From the day she met him, everything seemed to go wrong. She found she was always trying to save him by ringing him all the time, wanting to know where he was so that she could control him and keep him out of harm's way. This did not go down well for her with Ricky, as he was a free spirit, and before too long he left her for another woman.

Heartbroken, she came to me for a reading, hoping that I would give her some clarity and help her pick up the pieces. As soon as she sat down opposite me, her maternal grandmother came through in spirit and told her to let Ricky go because he was not good for her. Rachel knew this on some level, but she was still getting over the break-up. When it came to the reading, she had the Moon card in her career section. When I spoke to her about this, she said she was thinking of finally getting her own business going. She wanted to leave her job, which she found boring, and wanted to start a new life.

Straight away I told her to wait, as it was not the right time and it would be best if she held on to her job for at least another six months. This way she would be able to process her own life to date, take a well-deserved holiday, and spend some well-deserved *me* time. When I threw some more cards over the section, they clarified what I had originally said, and I could see her opening up her new place by the end of the year.

20) **The Sun (Clarity, Optimism, Renewed Trust)**

- A time of clarity, optimism, and renewed trust.
- Good times are coming; time for you to spread your wings.
- This is a time of rapid growth and incredible expansion in every aspect of your life.
- Hello happy days and goodbye to hard times.
- In No. 1 position—A great personality.

- In No. 4 position—A lovely house.
- In No. 10 position—A wonderful career.

This is a welcome time of clarity, optimism, and renewed trust in your world. It is now possible to understand your life, plan for the future, and move forward. You now have the foresight of purpose in your life, and it is time for you to believe in the striving human spirit moving you towards all your heart's desires and goals.

Case Study

Peggy was having trouble bringing her mother out from China to live with her in her lovely home in Australia. Her elderly mother was a widow who had been sick for some time and needed special care. Being the only child, Peggy felt guilty and was convinced it was her responsibility to look after her mother. Her mother did not want to come out, as she had lived most of her life in Hong Kong and had many friends there.

When Peggy came for the reading, her late father came into the room in spirit and starting saying how difficult Peggy's mum was and that she would soon find a new place in Hong Kong instead, a place where she would feel much better. He thanked her for being a good daughter but said she should not think it was her duty because if she brought her mother to Australia to live, there would be nothing but difficulties.

For a start her mother spoke no English. She was too old to be taken away from her loved ones, and she knew no one in Australia and would probably feel very lonely. When we did the spread, the Sun card came up immediately in the reading, and I told her no matter how difficult it all seemed at the moment, things would work out in her favor, as life always had a way of giving us different solutions to our problems.

A few days later Peggy rang me and said she had no second thoughts after she had talked to her father in spirit. She now agreed to let her mother stay in Hong Kong, as her aunty (who was very wealthy), wanted her mother to stay with her in her own apartment. Her aunty had a maid and felt that she should stay with her, as they always did so much together. Peggy was told she could visit any time.

21) **Judgment (Spiritual Rewards)**

- Spiritual contract and good karma; get ready to reap the benefits of good things coming your way.
- The individual now has the wisdom and spiritual insight to make the right choices in life; open the heart to new possibilities.
- In No. 10 position—Career changes; right job but changes coming.
- In No. 1 position—Switched-on spiritual person; trustworthy.

When the Judgment card appears in a spread, it indicates a time of rewards for past efforts will appear. It is a clear indication of how true we have been to ourselves. This is a period of summation, a realization of what we have been doing and where we have created the future that now awaits us.

This is a time of spiritual harvest, and the mistakes and creative efforts of the past are gathered together to form the future. This card may also mean the end of a chapter with beautiful new experiences just about to enter your life.

Case Study

Jane had worked hard in her energy healing and natural therapies practice. She had studied for many years so she could help the people around her and make a small business out of the work she loved so much. She was a very spiritual person, a born medium, and in my eyes an *earth angel* in every sense of the word, as she was always helping everyone around her. Her trouble was that many people often took advantage of her kindness, and she was her own worst enemy, as she had a habit of lending money and giving all her time and energy to those less worthy of her friendship and gentle nature.

Over the years this behavior became a pattern, as she had no idea logically who was good or bad. When these so-called friends had taken all they could, she ended up never seeing them again. When she came to see me for a reading, a spirit woman who said she was her grandmother came in for the reading. Her grandmother had loved her dearly and said not to lose faith, as things were really going to change around her. She also said that she was finally on the right path and not to worry because not only would she get plenty of work in her new practice but she would also travel overseas and run workshops.

When I pulled some cards out in the reading, the Judgment card came out. The other cards around it indicated that she would be working for a promoter and be travelling overseas as I also saw a lot of money coming in. When the reading was over, I told Jane that all good things came to those who waited. In Jane's case she was on her way to a wonderful windfall, and her gifts were now being recognized in a really big way.

22) **World (Success Card)**

- The world is your oyster!
- A time of completion and success is now entering the individual's life.
- In No. 10 position—Lots of success; things coming together.
- In No. 1 position—Connected to heaven; very spiritual.

When the World card appears in a spread, it means a time of great achievement and integration is coming. This is a period of triumph at the successful conclusion of a matter or the reaching of a goal that has been worked hard for and that ultimately leads to the birth of the Fool and so the circle, like the World, is complete.

Case Study

Angie was a writer and had written many books and articles over the years. Ever since she could remember she was always making up stories and writing things down even as a child. At the time I met her she was working for a busy magazine but was becoming concerned that there was no place to grow. She was still young and restless and wanted to work overseas. When she was a child, her parents immigrated to Australia, but she always felt like she never fitted in here and always had a dream of going back to London and working as an editor for a famous magazine.

As soon as she came into the room, an older woman came in as well in spirit and said she was her late aunt, who had been a brilliant newspaper editor many years ago. It was strange how this spirit came in because when I told Angie, she said she was not surprised, as she often felt her aunt around in spirit and felt she was the main influence for her wanting to be a writer most of her life.

When I pulled the tarot cards, the Wheel of Fortune came straight out, and I saw she had really good karma around her and that she would get an offer to work overseas in a company in London where she would do very well. That was many years ago, and I have since heard from Angie, who is now married to a lovely Englishman and who works as an editor for a world-renowned fashion magazine.

Minor Arcana Cards

There are fifty-six cards in the Minor Arcana. These are pentacles, wands, cups, and swords.

While the Major Arcana card meanings reveal events that will naturally occur because of the laws of destiny, karma, or the universe, the Minor Arcana cards reveal events in the person's life that happen naturally because of the laws of human nature. Minor Arcana cards highlight the more practical aspects of our life, referring to current issues and everyday occurrences that have only a minor influence in our lives. With these cards it us up to the individuals how they handle them.

The Minor Arcana Cards Have Four Suits

Pentacles are *money cards.* This suit signifies matters to do with finance, material possessions, business transactions, and career. Astrologically these are associated with earth signs (Capricorn, Virgo, and Taurus).

Wands are *work cards.* Wands represent ideas, communication, energy, social issues, and inspiration. Astrologically these are associated with fire signs (Aries, Leo, and Sagittarius).

Cups are *love/emotion cards.* They represent emotions, which may be good or bad, family matters, love, romance, our feelings, and our creativity. Astrologically these are associated with water signs (Pisces, Scorpio, and Cancer).

Swords are *intellect cards.* They represent power, thought, and the intellect. Sometimes these cards can indicate serious issues. Astrologically these are associated with air signs (Libra, Aquarius, and Gemini).

Page cards have dual meanings (Page of Pentacles, Page of Wands, Page of Cups, and Page of Swords). Normally they represent restlessness, new beginnings, and subtle changes, but they also indicate a young person.

People Cards in the Minor Arcana

Pentacles

King of Pentacles

Queen of Pentacles

Knight of Pentacles

Page of Pentacles (dual meaning)

King of Pentacles (Earth Sign—Capricorn, Virgo, or Taurean Male)

- May have qualities that represent the earth signs of Capricorn, Virgo, or Taurus.

- Earth sign male characteristics are that he loves his comforts, is materialistic, likes food, enjoys sex, is hard-working, and is usually confident and intelligent.
- Age usually indicates someone from thirty-five years old and upwards.
- Financially strong (pentacles in card).
- Likes to be in charge; would love to own or already owns a business; appreciates money.
- Taurean's have a tendency to be stubborn.
  - o Very methodical; don't like change.
  - o Earth sign male; very visual, sensual, and enjoys the pleasures in life.
- Capricorns are very methodical.
  - o Hard workers. Usually very focused on work.
  - o Grounded.
  - o But if they are out of sync, they can go to extremes.
- *Virgos* can be quite fixed and have a tendency to be controlling.

In the Circle Spread

- In No. 1 position—They like their material comforts; money; masculine.
- In No. 5 position—Ask the question "Have you met someone yet?" If so, they like money, have the Midas touch, and could be a Virgo, Capricorn, or Taurus.
- In No. 10 position—The person has someone around them that likes money, is earthy, or would work for someone like that.

When the King of Pentacles appears in a spread, it is time for the person to encounter the materialistic in his or her physical world. The King of Pentacles may enter someone's life as a very strong, successful, well-respected man, someone who might have what is called the *Midas touch* (meaning that everything he does turns to gold or that he is good with making money). This person, often through hard work and focus, has the gift of manifesting material things in the world. This card may also mean that the person is now ready to manifest material things in the world because he or she is focused, believe in him or herself, and know what he or she wants and how to get it.

Queen of Pentacles (Earth Sign—Capricorn, Virgo, or Taurean Female)

- Female version of the King of Pentacles.
- She is an earth sign with the qualities of a Capricorn, Virgo, or Taurus woman.
- Practical, earthy female.
- She is successful; likes to runs her own show; has to be the boss.
- Work-oriented.
- Strongly independent.
- Financially independent.
- Strong-minded, but can be very fixed or stubborn at times.
- Likes to be in control.
- Can be any age, but not a child.
- Sensual, sexy, and loves material things.

In the Circle Spread

- Very methodical.
- In No. 2 position—Can be good with money; knows how to make money work.
- In No 6 position—She knows how to look after herself but may be prone to laziness or excess.

When the Queen of Pentacles appears in people's readings, it is time to learn about themselves and their unique expressions of sensuality. These people are usually honest, mature, and reliable, and they have a firm understanding and appreciation of the materialistic world they live in. The Queen of Pentacles is an earthy, strong, sensual woman, usually self-sufficient and hard-working, who appreciates the material world and the beauty that is around her. This may also emerge as qualities for the person having the reading.

Knight of Pentacles (Earth Sign—Capricorn, Virgo, or Taurean Male)

- Younger man.
- Earth sign—Capricorn, Virgo, or Taurus.
- Some may think he is very easy-going, maybe boring at times, because he seems predictable.
- Loves food, sex, bodily pleasures; can be set in his ways; adventurous.
- Not as established as King of Pentacles.
- Humble, gentle, and hard-working.

When the Knight of Pentacles appears in a spread, it means someone is easy-going, grounded, and comfortable with himself. The young Knight of Pentacles may also be seen as quiet, intelligent, focused, down-to-earth, uncomplicated, industrious, humble, gentle, and hard-working but sometimes may also be seen as stubborn.

Page of Pentacles (Dual Meaning Card, Earth Sign—Capricorn, Virgo, or Taurus Child) or Gentle New Beginnings around the Client

In the Circle Spread

- Meaning No. 1—New beginnings with money.
- Meaning No. 2—Young child of an earth Sign.
- In No. 4 position—Starting up business from home.
- In No. 11 position—Social relationships, new beginning with a friend, money making.

When the Page of Pentacles appears in a spread, it means the beginning of something new in the materialistic world, a golden opportunity perhaps. This means money is now available to take up something the person wants to do like invest in a small business or hobby that may lead to a career. With gentle patience, determination, time, focus, and care, this will manifest for his or her future if the person learns to take up the opportunity. It can also indicate a young child with an earth/sun sign.

Wands

King of Wands

Queen of Wands

Knight of Wands (dual meaning)

Page of Wands (dual meaning)

King of Wands (Fire Sign—Aries, Leo, or Sagittarius)

- Fire sign—Aries, Leo, or Sagittarius.
- Male from thirty-five years old and upwards.
- Exciting individuals; dogmatic.
- Aries male—Stubborn; likes to be boss; enjoys nice things; competitive; controlling; a mover and a shaker; a go-getter.
- Sagittarius male—This man is always on the move and loves adventure and travel; very visual; unpredictable, like most fire signs.
- Leo male—This man loves his home. If you want to make him happy, tell him how good he looks or how nice his hair is.
- All these men are natural leaders and like to be in charge.

When the King of Wands appears in a spread, it can indicate a generous, kind-hearted man who is usually friendly to everyone. These types of signs make an excellent friend to both sexes, generate lots of energy, and often are full of ideas. This person is also a leader type but can sometimes be impatient and does not like to be told what to do.

Queen of Wands (Fire Sign—Aries, Leo, or Sagittarius)

- Fire sign—Aries, Leo, or Sagittarius.
- Dependable; strong; individual; passionate; fiery; very independent and likes to run her own show and be the star of it. They are usually extremely loyal and loving but can tend to fly off the handle if things don't go well. They make good friends, wives, and partners and like to talk to almost everyone.
- Leos and Aries like to be the queen of the home. Materialistic, they love to be surrounded by beautiful things, live in nice homes that are usually very beautiful, and they are proud of their houses. Friends must be loyal. If not, they are able to move on very fast.
- Sagittarius women are very social and would rather go out to eat instead of making dinner at home; too many things happening in their lives; very strong.

In the Circle Spread

- In No. 6 position—Strong and robust; on the go all the time.
- In No. 1 position—A very fiery person who is loyal and likes to take the lead. A very trusting individual but someone who knows when to move on.

When the Queen of Wands appears in a spread, it is usually indicating a woman who is a born leader and full of energy and ideas. She is often passionate, independent, loyal, and very creative. She is often seen as extremely imaginative and a magnetic person who likes to do her own thing but is full of compassion and warmth for others around her. She has a lust for life but can often be impatient. This woman loves to earn her own money and loves her home and family.

Knight of Wands (Dual Meaning Card, Fire Sign—Aries, Leo, or Sagittarius)

- Meaning No. 1—Sudden changes.
- Meaning No. 2—Young fire sign male less than thirty-five years old.

In the Circle Spread

- In No. 4 position—Moving house.
- In No. 10 position—leaving work within three months.
- In No. 2 position—Changes with finances (pull another card for details)
- Not as successful as King of Wands.

When the Knight of Wands appears in a spread, it is time for a change. This can mean a change of residence. (The card's position may also indicate what area of the subject's life will change.) Changes will occur wherever the individual suddenly feels too cramped by his or her environment, and he or she will seek broader and greener pastures.

This card may also indicate a young man entering the subject's life, one who is intense, charming with lots of charisma, honest and trustworthy, restless, exciting, and fun-loving. Stand back though because often this person can be slightly naïve, as he is full of new ideas that often may not be well developed.

Page of Wands (Dual Meaning Fire Sign—Aries, Leo, of Sagittarius)

- Meaning No. 1—Beginning of something new and creative.
- Meaning No. 2—Young fire sign person.
- *Restlessness of creative energy.*
  - o Gentle beginning with new work
  - o Study
  - o Creativity
  - o Intellectual
- Bringing in creative energy into life.

In the Circle Spread

- In No. 9 position—Restless; might be getting new guide.

When the Page of Wands appears in a spread, it is a signpost indicating something new is stirring in the subject's life. This may often manifest as restlessness at work, a vague feeling of dissatisfaction not yet strong enough to motivate a change, or a hint or a glimpse that one might be able to expand one's life in some way.

It can also mean a young child with the qualities of the wands.

Cups

King of Cups

Queen of Cups

Knight of Cups (dual meaning)

Page of Cups (dual meaning)

King of Cups (Water Sign—Pisces, Scorpio, or Cancer)

- Cup cards—emotional cards. Pisces, Scorpio, or Cancer male.
- Male of thirty-five years of age and upwards.
- Cancer male
  - o Secretive, moody; high achievers but hide it; sensitive, highly intuitive; like to be successful; home loving.
- Scorpio male
  - o Unforgiving if you've hurt them; sexual, passionate; intuitive; generous; secretive; closed book; materialistic; ambitious.

- Pisces male
  - o Dreamer; home loving, family oriented; creative in the arts; loving and affectionate.

When the King of Cups appears in a spread, it is time for the individual to experience the gifted counselor or the healer within. These men are very private, good-natured, fair, and passionate. They love to be attached or have partners, and they are extremely sensitive souls who are deeply emotional and quite intuitive. They make good parents, as they are family-oriented, love their children and their home, and usually have a love of the arts or music. They also like to be in control of their emotions and would never get involved too deeply with people they feel would threaten them in any way on an emotional level, as it takes them a long time to get over being hurt.

Queen of Cups (Water Sign—Pisces, Scorpio, or Cancer Female)

- Cup cards—emotional cards. Helen of Troy type. Pisces, Scorpio, or Cancer.
- Female of thirty-five years of age and upwards.
- You cross one of these signs, and they cut you off. *That's it!* And they don't come back for more.
- Pisces woman
  - o Very secretive, you never know where you stand with them; once they cut you off, it's over. Very sensitive; very romantic; good at what they do; easily hurt. Need to express themselves,

to speak up; artistic, intuitive, dreamers who fantasize. Elizabeth Taylor was a Pisces.

- Scorpio woman
  o Know what they want. A blonde Scorpio woman is different from a dark-haired one. Dark-haired is more laidback; the blonde is an ambitious, intuitive go-getter. If she is having problems in love, she is a wreck because she can't deal with heartbreak! These women are tenacious.
- Cancer woman
  o Home-loving; sensitive; easily hurt; dreamer; but when they get their act together, there is no stopping them.

The Queen of Cups may enter one's life as a mysterious, very private, hypnotic woman, not necessarily overtly seductive yet strangely disturbing. She can be a catalyst for the emergence of deep feelings and fantasies that were previously hidden from awareness. She is generally intuitive, highly secretive, artistic, and very creative. She loves beautiful things, may be a dreamer, but is often regarded as a great friend or counselor to people she allows in her inner circle. She is also very guarded and selective about those she allows into her circle of friendships and may take some time to get to know. She is also highly ambitious but likes to keep her own counsel, as her emotions run very deeply, and like the male of her type, she takes a long time to get over past hurts.

Knight of Cups (Dual Meaning Card, Water Sign—Pisces, Scorpio, or Cancer Male)

- Meaning No. 1—Young Pisces, Scorpio, or Cancer male who is very romantic, artistic, and a dreamer.
- Meaning No. 2—Proposition, offer, or contract that is artistic and/or exciting.

In the Circle Spread

- In No. 1 position—Person is artistic (artist card).
- In No. 4 position—Contract to buy house.
- In No. 5 position—Prince on a white horse (or romantic person or energy about to enter the subject's life).

When the Knight of Cups appears in a spread, it is time for the individual to experience romantic love, such as a proposal of marriage, an engagement, or simply falling in love. It can also indicate a charming, dreamy young man looking for adventure, someone who is poetic, sensitive, and under thirty-five.

Page of Cups (Dual Meaning Card, Water Sign—Pisces, Scorpio, or Cancer Male)

- Meaning No. 1—Young Pisces, Scorpio, or Cancer. Also birth of a child.
- Meaning No. 2—New relationship, and a new capacity to love.

In the Circle Spread

- In No. 1 position—Person is going within and needs to be gentle with themselves.
- In No. 4 position—House or home gives you pleasure.
- In No. 5 position—Beginning of love affair with Water sign.
- In No. 10 position—New job coming.

When the Page of Cups appears in a spread, the birth of something new on the feeling level is suggested. This might be a new relationship, a new quality of feeling within a relationship, or even the birth of a child. Often the Page of Cups means a renewal of the capacity to love, beginning with the love of self. It can also mean a young child of one of these star signs or qualities like it.

Swords

King of Swords

Queen of Swords

Knight of Swords (dual meaning)

Page of Swords (dual meaning)

King of Swords (Air Sign—Libra, Aquarius, or Gemini Male)

- Male of thirty-five years and upwards.
- Lovers of beauty.
- Rule with intellect.
- Very charming
- Likes order.
- Problem making decisions.
- Harmony and peace.
- Restless minds, always on the go!
- Politician, policeman, man in uniform, lawyer.
- Leader.
- In control.

When the King of Swords appears in a spread, it is time to meet the qualities of intellectual leadership, mental gifts, and strategies within yourself. These include intellectual prowess and inspired ideas about how to develop things in the future. This man is a leader type. He is usually in a position of authority, or he wears a uniform. Perhaps he is a lawyer or a politician. He is fair-minded and hard-working. He lives in his head, and he likes to call the shots.

Queen of Swords (Air Sign—Libra, Aquarius, or Gemini Female)

- Never misses a trick.
- Has a sharp tongue and doesn't take any nonsense.
- Mind is always on the go!

- Nice, kind.
- Lots of energy.
- Inquisitive.
- Sensitive.
- Very intellectual, good with mind.
- Do the wrong thing by them, and you'll get your fingers cut off.
- Don't cross them because they will investigate.
- Brain never stops working.
- May have problems making decisions and like to take their time when doing things.

When the Queen of Swords appears in a spread, she is seen as a strong-minded, intelligent woman who is a born leader. She may appear as idealistic, independent, and aloof. She is often accustomed to adversity and not afraid to confront difficult issues. A deep thinker, she may be an academic. She has little tolerance for the injustice she may see in people's lives around her or those who cross her path.

Knight of Swords (Dual Meaning Card, Air Sign—Libra, Aquarius, or Gemini)

- Meaning No. 1—Sudden changes coming in a certain month (an air sign month).
- Meaning No. 2—Young man.

In the Circle Spread

- In No. 1 position—Restless, always on the go!

- In No. 7 position—Restlessness within marriage. (Pull another card for more details.)

When the Knight of Swords appears in a spread, it is time for the individual to prepare for sudden changes that will break apart the ordinary patterns of life. This card may also indicate a young man under thirty-five with the qualities of the star signs, a young man who may be seen as a risk-taker and someone who loves adventure.

Page of Swords (Dual Meaning Card, Air Sign—Libra, Aquarius, or Gemini)

- Meaning No. 1—People talking about you or the subject.
- Meaning No. 2—Changing the way you think (the reason they are talking about you).
- Gossip card.
- Negative card.
- A young child with the qualities of the star sign.

In the Circle Spread

- In No. 6 position—Health problems.
- In No. 10 position—Problems at work.

When the Page of Swords appears in a spread, it is a warning card, as it can mean potential gossip, spying, or something of a secretive nature around you. You are changing within and beginning to think in another way others may not be used to.

Pentacles (Money Cards, Cards with Coins, Represent Money)

Ace of Pentacles to Ten of Pentacles

The majority of the Pentacles cards reflect a time of abundance and prosperity. The suit of pentacles develops material success.

- Ace of Pentacles—New beginnings with finances.
- Two of Pentacles—Balance with money.
- Three of Pentacles—Small rewards; timing card.
- Four of Pentacles—Holding too tightly onto things.
- Five of Pentacles—Loss; grief; low self-esteem.
- Six of Pentacles—The recipient of generosity.
- Seven of Pentacles—Careful decisions to be made, usually around money.
- Eight of Pentacles—Apprentice; honing your craft.
- Nine of Pentacles—Success; achievement; rewards.
- Ten of Pentacles—Great success; great achievement.

Ace of Pentacles

- New beginnings with finances.
- Coming into money.
- More money coming to you.
- Might get a pay rise.

In the Circle Spread

- In No. 1 position—Person is good at attracting money.
- In No. 10 position—Very good job; attracts money at work; is good at what they do.
- In No. 8 position—Might come into some money.

The Ace of Pentacles generally indicates material achievement in the physical world because energy is now available. It often indicates money or a new type of work becoming available. Everything may seem to be coming up roses in the material world.

Two of Pentacles (Earth Sign—Capricorn, Virgo, or Taurus Male)

- Balance with money card.
- A little bit of fluctuation/balance with money likely means finances will improve.

Two of Pentacles heralds a time when money and energy are likely to be available for new projects. There is a need for balance, as there may be turbulence as you juggle your income. On a positive note it may be a welcome card to those who know how to *play* with money.

Three of Pentacles

- Small rewards and timing card.

- Small rewards are coming.
- Timing card—Three days, weeks, months, or years.

The Three of Pentacles usually means early success in some material you have been pursuing, material recognition, or a reward for a job well done. A creative project you have been working on may earn profits, such as a book that shows early success in the market. This is a time when you are not seeing the final outcome as the project is really just beginning on its journey.

Four of Pentacles

- Holding on too tightly to things.

In the Circle Spread

- In No. 1 position—This person can be uptight. He or she holds on to things too much. He or she is unwilling to let go, and the problem is usually with money. If he or she holds on to his or her money, they will most likely hold on to other things.

The Four of Pentacles warns about an attitude of holding on too tightly to things that are bound up with the sense of self-worth. But this person knows the value of money.

Five of Pentacles

- Loss; grief; a small setback; low self-esteem.
- Low self-esteem; not much happening; at a loss or the person is lost.
- Can also mean loss of employment.

The Five of Pentacles usually means a period of financial difficulty or loss. This may also mean the loss of confidence and faith in one's self. This is a time to stand back, go within, and reflect for a better outcome. This can also mean temporary loss of income, a decline in lifestyle and self-respect, or the need for assistance from a charitable or welfare society.

Six of Pentacles

- Recipient of generosity; able to assist others if need be.
- The victory card in any situation.
- People being generous; the receipt of generosity from the universe.

In the Circle Spread

- In No. 6 position—Support from people; good influence with nutrition.
- In No. 10 position—Generous boss and colleagues.
- In No. 11 position—Generous friends.

The Six of Pentacles indicates a situation where there is money or substance to be shared, where the individual will be called upon to offer generosity or be the recipient of another's generosity. Faith in life and in his or her own capacities is regained. This is a time for happiness, as it is the victory card in any situation.

Seven of Pentacles

- Careful decisions to be made, usually around money.
- Slow but steady rise in income.
- Need to pull another card to see the outcome.

In the Circle Spread

- In No. 6 position—This is an opportunity to get healthy, so go for it, or else you will have health problems.
- In No. 9 position—If you decide to meditate, a new guide could be coming in; the reader could ask if the subject has been working on themselves spiritually.

The Seven of Pentacles means a time when a difficult work decision must be made. Care and forethought are needed, and the question arises of whether to continue to develop what one has already built or to put energy into a new project instead.

Eight of Pentacles

- Apprentice card or new job.
- Ability to work on themselves, finding out who they are. Going through life change; lots of possibilities.
- A person will only get back what he or she puts in.

The Eight of Pentacles can indicate a period when the individual plays the role of the hard-working apprentice. This card can suggest a talent that the individual has recently discovered and that is worthy of development and effort. It can also imply that a hobby could be developed into a profession.

Nine of Pentacles

- Success; achievement; rewards.
- This card is about working very hard for achievement and receiving great satisfaction.

In the Circle Spread

- In No. 2 position—Very successful, right on track.
- In No. 9 position—Great satisfaction and rewards, as they have a good connection to their higher self and guides that are working with them.
- In No. 7 position—Good marriage, everything is on track.
- In No. 6 position—This indicates that they have really good health

- In No. 11 position—The person has great friends who are very supportive.

The Nine of Pentacles means that the luxuries of life are now available at the individual's fingertips. The person should feel pleased with themselves, as he or she can enjoy the hard-earned fruits of his or her labor with pleasure and satisfaction.

Ten of Pentacles

- Great success; great achievement.
- Similar to the World card in the Major Arcana; even better than Nine of Pentacles card.
- Ongoing contentment and security.
- An exciting card to pick.
- Rubbing your hands together with joy and excitement.

In the Circle Spread

- In No. 10 position—Career success.

The Ten of Pentacles suggests a period of ongoing contentment and security. There is a sense of something permanent having been established, something that can be handed on to others. This is a time for artistic or material rewards. This often signals an achievement of some kind, perhaps around a contract, book, or painting. It can also mean one will get the go-ahead with some project.

Cups (Love, Emotion, Relationship Cards, Cards with Cups, Represent Emotions)

Ace of Cups to Ten of Cups

The majority of the cups cards reflect the person's emotions.

- Ace of Cups—A Big awakening of your heart.
- Two of Cups—Spiritual contract.
- Three of Cups—Celebrations.
- Four of Cups—Restlessness; dissatisfaction; boredom.
- Five of Cups—Betrayal.
- Six of Cups—Nostalgia.
- Seven of Cups—Choice.
- Eight of Cups—Emotional changes.
- Nine of Cups—Wish card.
- Ten of Cups—Love and relationships success.

Ace of Cups

- Big awakening of your heart.
- Peace of mind and personal happiness.
- Totally in love and nothing makes sense. Brain has turned to mush. Everything feels, looks, and appears wonderful and dreamlike.

The Ace of Cups generally means an outpouring of feeling. It is often raw, vital, and overwhelming. Romance in its greatest form will now be knocking at your door. This card may mean the beginning of a new relationship in the client's life, as the person is now ready to embark on a journey of love.

Two of Cups

- Spiritual contract.
- Commitment, engagement, or a bond of some kind.
- Beginning of a relationship or reconciliation of an existing relationship.

In the Circle Spread

- In No. 3 position—Agreements/contracts with relatives. You were born into this family to learn lessons.
- In No. 5 position—Spiritual person coming into your life.
- In No. 10 position—You are on the right path, working with your spirituality at work.

Two of Cups usually indicates the beginning of a relationship. It can also mean contractual arrangements of business partners.

Three of Cups

- Celebrations card—Engagement, marriage, pregnancy, or similar.
- An exciting card.

The Three of Cups suggests the celebration of a marriage, the start of a love affair, a pregnancy, the birth of a child, or some other situation of emotional fulfillment and promise.

Four of Cups

- Restlessness; dissatisfaction; boredom.
- Fear of disappointment.
- Person needs to do some talking and planning.

The Four of Cups may mean a time of dissatisfaction, boredom, and depression within a relationship. There is a feeling of being let down or cheated, although they themselves are usually the ones who do the cheating because of their unread expectations. This dissatisfaction can lead to long-standing, unexpressed resentment, or it can lead to looking more deeply at a relationship, which is a harder path because previous assumptions and fantasies will be challenged.

Five of Cups

- Betrayal card.
- Often we betray ourselves by not listening to our intuition.
- A feeling of being unloved.
- Not a final ending, something can still be worked on.

The Five of Cups implies regret over past actions. Something has gone wrong. A betrayal has occurred, and there is sadness and remorse. Separation in a relationship can occur, and there is a fear of not being loved. The good thing is that this can be seen as a spiritual contract, as it is teaching personal responsibility so that the individual learns to take his or her power back.

Six of Cups

- Nostalgia card.
- Happy memories from childhood.
- Longing for the past.

In the Circle Spread

- In No. 1 position—Person is a daydreamer.
- In No. 5 position—Stuck in the past, thinking about past loves; maybe needs to let them go.

The Six of Cups can imply nostalgia about the past or living in the past, whereas living in the now is the only place where we can make our dreams and achievements happen.

Seven of Cups

- Choice card.
- Several opportunities may present themselves at once.
- Make the time to prioritize things that are important in your life.

In the Circle Spread

- In No. 4 position—Decision to stay or move on; thinking about moving on.
- Middle spread (the four cards)—Many choices coming up during the year.

The Seven of Cups signals an emotional situation in which much potential is evident but where the individual is faced with the challenge of choosing and acting in realistic terms to make that potential manifest. He or she must make those choices for him or herself.

Eight of Cups

- Emotional changes.

The Eight of Cups implies the necessity of giving something up on an emotional level and letting go of things or attachments. This may also be a temptation to pursue temporary distractions. This is a time to just let go and move on.

Nine of Cups

- The wish card.
- Dreams coming true.
- Emotional contentment.

In the Circle Spread

- In No. 1 position—Person who is successful and someone who was born under a lucky star, as she or she always attracts good luck.
- In No. 12 position—Good luck coming the subject's way; even though he or she may feel bad, good things are on the way.

The Nine of Cups is the wish card. It signals a time of all wishes coming true, with great joy and happiness. It indicates a time of celebration for past efforts and commitment to goals.

Ten of Cups

- Love and success in relationships.
- Ideal family conditions; emotional security.
- A state of permanent and ongoing contentment.

The Ten of Cups can indicate ongoing contentment, happiness, and blessings for the realm of the heart. This also means great family conditions.

Swords

These usually represent mental thoughts and conflict at times.

Ace of Swords to Ten of Swords

- Ace of Swords—Big, big changes.
- Two of Swords—At an impasse in your life.
- Three of Swords—Great heartache.
- Four of Swords—Contemplation time.
- Five of Swords—Learning to live within your limits.
- Six of Swords—Breakthrough.
- Seven of Swords—Usage of guile, tact, diplomacy, and wit.
- Eight of Swords—Absolutely stuck!
- Nine of Swords—Gloom and doom.
- Ten of Swords—Finishing card.

Ace of Swords

- Big, big change.
- Get out the sword and cut out the crap going on around them. Be like Archangel Michael getting out his sword and cutting all the ties.
- Ace card represents making big changes.

The Ace of Swords implies that some new creative viewpoint will emerge out of conflict. The hand of fate forces us to make decisions that bring victory and success. It is a time of waking up and making life changes so a new order can come.

Two of Swords

- Impasse or truce situation.
- Do nothing.

- Can't do anything, just stuck. There is a refusal to face some impending conflict.

In the Circle Spread

- In No. 1 position—Person can't make decisions.

The Two of Swords means a truce must be called for a situation that cannot be solved any other way.

Three of Swords

- Great heartache.
- Teary or dreary.
- Broken romance, heartbreak.

In the Circle Spread

- In No. 1 position—Person has emotional issues.
- In No. 6 position—Person is depressed.
- In No. 7 position—Not a good marriage.
- In No. 10 position—Things not good at work. (Pull another card for clarity.)

The Three of Swords means strife, conflict, or separation. This is like an abscess that has to be lanced so it can heal in time.

Four of Swords

- A time for contemplation.
- Time to rest.
- Quiet time of withdrawal and contemplation.
- A period of introversion, reflection; emotional recuperation after the outbreak of conflict.

In the Circle Spread

- In No. 1 position—Person is introspective.

The Four of Swords means quiet time, recuperation, and rest. When this card appears in a spread, it is perhaps wise to accept solitude or withdrawal and not seek to fill the time with activities. It is a time to go within to make order in life.

Five of Swords

- Living within your limits.
- Battles fought and won.
- Acceptance of limitation, boundaries, and the confines of destiny.

In the Circle Spread

- In No. 1 position—Person knows his or her boundaries.

The Five of Swords means facing and knowing your limits. It signals a need to recognize your own powers and capabilities before you move forward again.

Six of Swords

- Breakthrough card.
- Time when things will start to get better.
- Things might be a little rough at the moment but things will get smoother.
- Look at the card. The boat is in rough seas, but looking out further, the water is smooth.

The Six of Swords suggests a time to seek escape from turbulent times for the sake of peace of mind. One should stand back to escape from difficult circumstances at this time.

Seven of Swords

- Usage of guile, tact, diplomacy, and wit.
- Application of mental energy in a cautious, wily, and diplomatic way in order to gain the end desired.
- Someone false is around.
- Brains rather than brawn; life may require the individual to develop guile, wit, and cunning.

The Seven of Swords means a time when we need to be clever but keep our ideas and thoughts to ourselves. It is a time to use guile, tact, diplomacy, and wit. Sometimes life requires us to just sit back and *play the game* to achieve our own ends for a better outcome.

Eight of Swords

- Absolutely stuck!
- Feeling of complete helplessness.
- A situation of bondage through fear.
- This bondage involves full knowledge of the situation and the probable consequences of any choice.

The Eight of Swords refers to the time when an individual is unable to act because of his or her fear of the consequences. A decision is necessary, but either choice will lead to trouble. This also indicates the need to see how the individual has created this situation in his or her life.

Nine of Swords

- Gloom and doom.
- Nervous disorders; deep depression; possibly headaches or migraines.
- Experience of great fear and anxiety.
- Much fear going on in the person's life.

The Nine of Swords can mean a period of great anxiety and fear about future.

Ten of Swords

- Finishing card.
- Represents an ending where there may have been abuse, back-stabbing of the worst kind, or violence.
- Ending and finishing.
- Good things are coming.

The Ten of Swords heralds the final ending of a difficult situation. A new future can begin once it is let go, allowing new things to come

Wands (The Work and Career Cards)

Ace of Wands to Ten of Wands.

This signifies work, business, and career.

- Ace of Wands—New beginnings with work.
- Two of Wands—New ideas to do with work.
- Three of Wands—Timing card (to do with work).
- Four of Wands—Breakthrough or moving forward with work.
- Five of Wands—Financial problems.
- Six of Wands—Victory with work.
- Seven of Wands—Struggle.
- Eight of Wands—Overseas travel or fruitful progress.
- Nine of Wands—Exhaustion.
- Ten of Wands—Stress/budgie card.

Ace of Wands

- New beginnings with work.
- New career, new work.

This card means new beginnings with work or career. The Ace of Wands means an uprising of bubbling, creative energy. This may mean good news with work and new beginnings in the work department.

Two of Wands

- New ideas to do with work.
- One idea leads to another, and often the first one is not the final one but merely a prelude for good things to come.
- A person who feels in control.

The Two of Wands means new aims, ideas, goals, or creative projects.

Three of Wands

- Timing card to do with work—three days/weeks/ months/years.
- Everything is well with work, but there are changes coming.

The Three of Wands implies a stage of initial completion of a creative idea or project. It may also serve as a time card. This card can also mean the material achievement of success at this stage of the journey.

Four of Wands

- Breakthrough or moving forward with work.
- Celebrations of security.
- Card of harvest and reward.
- The challenge of a new creative idea has been met. Hard work has been applied, and now the individual can reap the solid reward that has been earned through effort.

The Four of Wands means a time of reward for efforts made in the past.

Five of Wands

- Financial problems.
- Card represents struggle.
- Money troubles (shortage of funds, cash-flow problems).

In the Circle Spread

- In No. 1 position—self-pitying person, never has any money.
- In No. 6 position—Poor health.
- In No. 9 position—Not listening to intuition.

The Five of Wands means a time of struggle, arguments, and fighting. This is inner turmoil because of misunderstandings. Mundane matters may begin to go wrong. Compromises must be made while one retains the integrity of the original vision.

Six of Wands

- Victory card.
- Represents an experience of triumph, recognition by others, and public acclaim.
- A heady moment for the individual who has been striving to express some new idea or creative vision to others, for it is the moment of validation by the collective for the individual's efforts.

The Six of Wands means celebrations along with public acclaim or acknowledgement of some kind. This might take the form of a promotion, a qualification, or the recognition of some piece of creative work.

Seven of Wands

- Struggle card.
- The struggle here is an evenly matched contest of men against men.
- Somebody else wants what we have worked so hard to achieve, and we are plunged into a contest that challenges us to try even harder.
- The message is that we cannot rest on our laurels or someone will come along and steal our ideas.

The Seven of Wands means a struggle with other people's creative ideas or stiff competition. The individual is challenged to improve upon and develop his or her project in the face of an envious and competitive world. He or she needs to learn to value his or her ambition and competitive instinct.

Eight of Wands

- Dual meaning card—overseas travel or fruitful progress.
- Overseas travel.
- A release of creative energy after anxieties has been overcome. Conflict stimulates the imagination, and if this has been faced and worked through, there is often a period of smooth sailing where plans proceed towards the goal at a rapid rate and there is a feeling of buoyancy and confidence.

The Eight of Wands heralds a period of action after a delay or struggle. Travel is sometimes implied, or there is a clear stretch of fruitful creative activity where the imagination flows unchecked after anxieties and tensions have been overcome or resolved.

Nine of Wands

- Exhaustion card.
- Totally exhausted but still need to carry on.
- Struggling, but clear water can be seen.

- At this time the individual feels he or she simply cannot go on. His or her energy is all used up. His or her strength has gone, but it has all been for nothing.
- This card portrays the tremendous power of the creative imagination, for just when the individual feels he or she cannot fight one more battle or confront one more difficulty, somehow in the midst of this stress the ideas and the energy become available to take on this final challenge before one reaches the goal.

The Nine of Wands means a time when at the point of exhaustion a final challenge arises to prevent the individual from reaching his or her goal, and somehow, mysteriously he or she cannot find the strength in reserve to meet the challenge. This strength is only available when we have used up every other possibility, and it seems to be invoked by both the need and the willingness despite exhaustion to try one more time.

Ten of Wands

- Stress/the *budgie* card (imagine what it feels like to be stuck in a cage all day).
- A state of oppression; continual worries; exhaustion; insecurity; and stress.
- A person who double-checks everything constantly.
- The individual feels caught up in it all. This is a feeling of being totally overburdened, making it hard to even think of new things and difficult to move on.

The Ten of Wands means that the person may be overburdened and oppressed by having taken on more than he or she can deal with. This makes it difficult for the individual to even think, as he or she has too many concerns. Sometimes it is just best to stop what he or she is doing and wait until things start to move again.

LAYOUTS AND SPREADS

The circle spread is my favorite overall spread and reading to work with. Not only is it easy, but it gives a precise overall reading for a six-to-twelve-month period.

The Circle Spread

Position no. 1—Person/personality.

Position no. 2—Finances (money coming in through work or business generally).

Position no. 3—Relatives (people who are close to you, family, or close friends).

Position no. 4—Home (the home environment).

Position no. 5—Marriage/partnerships (relationships around the person).

Position no. 6—Health (a general look to see what is going on).

Position no. 7—Marriage/partnerships (to do with love and partnerships).

Position no. 8—Sex/death/regeneration (what the person is going through at the time of the reading. This goes with position 12, hidden things in the person's life.)

Position no. 9—The higher-self or higher consciousness, super conscious mind, or intuition.

Position no. 10—The career section.

Position no. 11—Social relationships.

Position no. 12—Hidden things the person may not be aware of.

Note that cards eight and twelve are read together in the reading.

Cards one to four, placed in the centre of the circle, refer to overall reading.

Add more cards on top until you have a positive outcome.

We are only looking for positive outcomes. If there is a negative card, keep going to reassure the client all will be well and look for a positive outcome.

The Circle Spread

One card spread using a card from
the Major Arcana Tarot

Three Card Spread

Past	Present	Future
1	2	3

Five Card Spread

Past	Present	Obstacles
1	2	3

Incoming Influences	Future
4	5

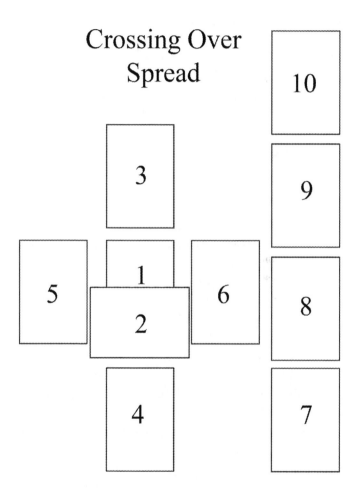

Crossing Over
Spread

Notes on the Spreads

I always keep two sets of cards—one for myself and the other for my clients. I store them in a box or wrap them up. When I use them, I always tap them and send white light to them with love before I start shuffling. After I have finished doing this, I will either let my client pull three cards or will pull the cards myself.

1) The circle spread is my favorite all-rounder, as it will give you a general outlook at what is going on in the subject's life. I use this spread all the time with my students and my clients. It is never wrong. It can be used for a three—or six-month spread or one year. The readers can keep pulling cards from the pack once they are on a house to get more information.

2) The one-card spread is the destiny or karma card. Some people like to call it *God's will* card. When this card is pulled, it indicates where the subject is meant to be in his or her life at this moment with his or her contracts and lessons here on Earth, which spirit calls *a large stage in the lessons of life.* Just shuffle the cards and pick one out of the twenty-two Major Arcana cards from the pack.

3) The three-card spread is very simple. Shuffle your cards, ask a question, and then pick out three cards from the pack. The first card is the past, the second the present, and the third is the outcome.

4) The five-card spread gives more information. Shuffle the cards and then place them in their positions. The first card is the passing influences

or where the subject has come from or has learnt. The second card is the present-day card or where the person is now. The third card shows any obstacles or blockages stopping the subject from moving forward. The fourth card shows incoming influences that are yet to happen, and the fifth card reveals the future or where the person will end up.

5) The crossing-over spread gives a complex yet simple read for the next three months. The first card is the person. The second card is the influences around that person at the moment. The third is what is blocking him or her. The fourth card is the support he or she has around him or her at this time. The fifth card represents the past. The sixth card shows the new future. The seventh card is how the individual ends up. The eighth card reveals hopes and fears. The ninth card tells us how the world sees the person, and the tenth card indicates the future or what happens.

Spiritual Medium, Clairvoyant and International Author

Kerrie Erwin

WWW.PUREVIEW.COM.AU

Sydney-based medium Kerrie has lived between two worlds since childhood and is able to *see* and *hear* spirit people talking. Realizing her true calling when she was very young, she now works professionally as a spiritual medium and clairvoyant, working with spirit rescue and hauntings and connecting people to loved ones who have passed over into the spirit world. She also teaches metaphysics and reads tarot cards. She is trained in spiritual hypnotherapies and past-life regression.

Closely aligned to her healing work is Kerrie's vibrant creative nature, as she regularly works on stage and in spiritualist churches around the country. Kerrie has also written several books, has worked on radio, and is a highly sought-after writer. She regularly contributes to publications and magazines, and she has written several articles on the paranormal over the years for *Insight* magazine and *Women's Day*.

Coming from a media background, she has also hosted her own show on cable TV called *Let's Have a Chat with Kerrie* on CVT-1 cable television. Her aim as a spiritual medium is to help as many people as possible, to teach others that love is eternal, to grow, and to inspire others to believe in themselves. She currently works on *Psychic TV* in Australia. Her books to date are *Magical Tales of the Forest*, *Memoirs of a Suburban Medium*, and *Spirits Whispering in My Ear*. These books are now available to buy on her website, at selected bookstores, and also as e-books on Kindle and Amazon.